TENNESSEE WILLIAMS

A Study of the Short Fiction

Twayne's Studies in Short Fiction

Gordon Weaver, General Editor
Oklahoma State University

Tennessee Williams.
Photograph by Sam Shaw, courtesy of New Directions Publishing Corp.

TENNESSEE WILLIAMS

A Study of the Short Fiction

Dennis Vannatta
University of Arkansas at Little Rock

TWAYNE PUBLISHERS • BOSTON
A Division of G. K. Hall & Co.

Twayne's Studies in Short Fiction Series No. 4
Editorial Assistant to Gordon Weaver: Stephanie Corcoran

Copyright © 1988 by G. K. Hall & Co.
All rights reserved.
Published by Twayne Publishers
A Division of G. K. Hall & Co.
70 Lincoln Street, Boston, Massachusetts 02111

Copyediting supervised by Barbara Sutton.
Book design and production by Janet Zietowski.
Typeset in 10/12 Caslon by Compset, Inc.

Printed on permanent/durable acid-free paper
and bound in the United States of America.

Library of Congress Cataloging-in-Publication Data

Vannatta, Dennis P.
  Tennessee Williams : a study of the short fiction / Dennis Vannatta.
    p.   cm. — (Twayne's studies in short fiction : TSSF 4)
  Bibliolography: p.
  Includes index.
  ISBN 0-8057-8304-0 (alk. paper)
  1. Williams, Tennessee, 1911–1983—Fictional works. I. Title.
II. Series.
PS3545.I5365Z857   1988
813'.54—dc19
                                                    88-10977
                                                    CIP

Contents

Preface

Commenting on his sudden rise to prominence as America's leading playwright in the late 1940s, Tennessee Williams often spoke of the "catastrophe of success." He was referring to fame's assault on his always precarious emotional health and his increasing difficulty in dealing with personal relationships, himself, life. Another casualty of this catastrophe, however, has been not so much his reputation as his *acknowledgment* as a short story writer. Along with any number of other figures in literary history, Williams is victim of the understandable but regrettable tendency among readers and critics to become so blinded by the writer's brilliance in one genre that they overlook perhaps lesser but certainly worthy accomplishments in another. Everyone knows Emily Brontë to be the author of *Wuthering Heights*, but how many know her to be one of the finer woman poets of the nineteenth century? Everyone acknowledges Samuel Beckett to be one of the preeminent playwrights of the contemporary period, but how many are aware of the possibility that his most significant contribution is in the novel?

This tendency is exacerbated in regard to the short story, which, with little logic, has too frequently been thought of as an apprentice genre, preparation for more serious pursuits. Perhaps the most ludicrous example is a newspaper headline announcing the death of Jorge Luis Borges, "Argentine, novelist"[1] (who, let it be known, never wrote a novel in his life but was one of history's great short story writers).

Criticism of Williams's writing is voluminous, but it runs probably fifty to one—a very rough guess—concerning the plays rather than the short stories. In his fine biography, *The Kindness of Strangers: The Life of Tennessee Williams*, Donald Spoto discusses all of Williams's full-length plays, even the late failures, in some detail, but does not so much as mention the publication of any of Williams's collections of short stories. When Spoto does turn his attention to individual short stories, it is almost always to show the relationship between a story and a play or to show how some incident from Williams's life turns up in a story. Very rarely does Spoto discuss a story because of its intrinsic aesthetic merits; in any case, he almost never devotes more than a single paragraph to a story.

This general neglect of Williams's short fiction would be more understandable were his talents in that genre meager. On the contrary, Spoto himself notes that several of Williams's short stories will "perhaps be recognized as masterpieces of that genre."[2] In his introduction to Williams's *Collected Stories*, Gore Vidal observes that Williams "has a narrative tone of voice that is totally compelling. The only other American writer to have this gift was Mark Twain."[3] Williams published four collections of short stories during his lifetime. His posthumous *Collected Stories* (1985) includes forty-nine stories, nine previously unpublished. Prior to collection his stories appeared in such august periodicals as the *New Yorker, Esquire, Mademoiselle, Antaeus,* and *Story* and were anthologized in three of the *Best American Short Stories* annuals and elsewhere.

It is not the thesis of this study that Williams is a better short story writer than playwright. Williams is frequently acclaimed as America's greatest playwright; he is universally acclaimed as being among the top two or three. But Williams began writing and publishing short fiction before he began writing plays, and he continued to publish interesting short stories long past the time when his plays had degenerated to, at their worst, the virtually unperformable. A few, at least, of his stories seem destined to survive the test of time, and a score of them are highly imaginative, entertaining, moving works. Williams deserves to be recognized as a fine short story writer as well as a great playwright; at the very least, his stories deserve to be read.

One other reason for reading and discussing Williams's short stories should be mentioned here. Along with the growth and visibility of gay activist groups in the sixties and seventies came the charge that Williams failed to deal honestly and directly in his plays with the issue of homosexuality—although he certainly discussed his homosexuality openly and, one might almost say, gleefully in interviews and especially in his *Memoirs* (1975). From as early as 1941 (the writing of "The Mysteries of the Joy Rio"), however, Williams was writing sensitive and interesting short fiction in which homosexuality is an issue; and the subject becomes more frequently and directly dramatized over the remainder of his short-fiction career. If we wish, then, to see how a great writer dealt artistically with this very personal, often painful, part of his life, we must turn to his short fiction.

Especially since several of Williams's stories served as prototypes for some of his greatest plays, the temptation is great to focus disproportionate attention on the relationship between the two genres. Such is not the aim of this study, however. Rather, the plays will be mentioned only insofar as they shed light on the stories. The aim of this study is twofold: to locate the Williams constants—those concerns, themes, character types, technical strategies, and so on that characterize his short fiction—and to trace the development of and variations on those constants over the course of a long career. Where atypical elements appear, of course, these too will be discussed.

A second temptation is perhaps harder to avoid than that of focusing disproportionate attention on the plays. Donald Spoto says that Williams was "a man more disturbing, more dramatic, richer and more wonderful than any character he ever created,"[4] the type of claim that we usually can dismiss as biographer's hyperbole. In this case, however, the evidence supports the biographer. Williams was so brilliant, flamboyant, complex, and tortured that the temptation to focus more attention on him than on his works is great. This temptation generally manifests itself in the scholar favoring those stories that can be interpreted biographically—to the detriment of other, perhaps finer, efforts. In this study, however, the facts of Williams's life will be alluded to only insofar as they help illuminate the works. I am indebted to Donald Spoto's fine biography for most of my information on Williams's life, and readers who turn to *The Kindness of Strangers: The Life of Tennessee Williams* will find their attention richly rewarded.

Literary history will probably place Williams the short story writer in the Southern-Gothic tradition, along with Flannery O'Connor, Eudora Welty, Carson McCullers, Truman Capote, and others. His best efforts, especially, recall McCullers's fiction (or hers, his). But Williams was, without question, a genius, and genius is characterized by being too large for the pigeonholes it helps to define. That "compelling voice" that Gore Vidal mentioned is as unmistakably Southern as any writer's, yet in Williams's best efforts locale is of marginal importance. Williams spent virtually all of his adult life in manic travel, after all, seeking something or fleeing something but never finding, never escaping; and his short fiction has the universality of pain and beauty, of cruelty, passion, and compassion, of love and death. Williams experienced it all, and he included it all in his writing.

Preface

Work on this study was facilitated by assistance from any number of people, to all of whom I am indebted. I would especially like to acknowledge the help and guidance of Gordon Weaver of Oklahoma State University and Anne Jones of Twayne Publishers. I am also grateful for permission to study materials in the Special Collection of the Elmer Ellis Library of the University of Missouri—Columbia and materials at the Harry Ransom Research Center, the University of Texas at Austin. Nor could this study have been completed without help from the interlibrary-loan staff at the University of Arkansas at Little Rock. Finally, my work with Tennessee Williams has made me realize just how painful a life spent depending on the kindness of strangers can be; accordingly, I am more grateful than ever that my wife and children have enabled me to escape that fate.

Dennis Vannatta

University of Arkansas at Little Rock

Notes

1. "Argentine, novelist, dies at 86," *Arkansas Gazette*, 15 June 1986, 12.
2. Donald Spoto, *The Kindness of Strangers: The Life of Tennessee Williams* (Boston: Little, Brown, 1985), 290.
3. Gore Vidal, introduction, *Tennessee Williams: Collected Stories* (New York: New Directions, 1985), xx.
4. Spoto, *Kindness of Strangers*, xviii.

Part 1

THE SHORT FICTION:
A CRITICAL ANALYSIS

Apprenticeship:
The Early Years (1928–40)

His name was not really Tennessee, of course; it was Thomas Lanier Williams. Nor was he from Tennessee; he neither was born nor lived there, except for two years in Nashville when he was too young to have remembered it and a few months with his grandparents in Memphis one summer. The nickname was hung on him at the University of Iowa by fellow students who could not remember just which of the Southern states this quiet young man with the broad accent was from.

The source of the nickname is not so important as the fact that Williams chose to keep it—he could have abandoned it at any point after leaving Iowa, obviously. Perhaps it represented for Williams a certain gentility, a golden age of sensibility and sociability that was lost when his family moved, in his seventh year, from small-town Mississippi to industrial, grimy, brutal St. Louis. Or perhaps in assuming the name, Williams was attempting to change an identity that was becoming increasingly disturbing to him. It probably will not do to make too much of the name, though. It was given in friendship and may have represented no more to Williams than affability fondly remembered. He depended heavily, after all—as his biographer, Donald Spoto, suggests—on the kindness of friends and strangers.

Tennessee Williams was the kindest, the most sensitive of men. He could also be cruel, insensitive, suspicious, and paranoid. He was generous and loving and elicited generosity and love from others. Many of those whom he loved the most and to whom he owed the most he hurt and rejected: his brother, Dakin, his longtime agent Audrey Wood, his lover Frank Merlo. The one person to whom he never wavered in his love and loyalty was his sister, Rose, who represented for him all the beauty and sensitivity that could blossom in the world and all the horrors that life could marshal against such vulnerability. Tennessee Williams loved life with an enormous passion and took his own. If we do not offically call it suicide, it is only because we hesitate to apply that term to a process of selfdestruction taking two decades to complete.

Williams was a man of contradictions and clashing passions, and so is his short fiction, which, claims Gore Vidal, constitutes "the true memoir of Tennessee Williams."[1] He was the most autobiographical of writers. If he thought it, felt it, or lived it, it would likely show up in his fiction either directly or indirectly. For this reason, although it is not the purpose of this study to provide extensive biographical data, a gloss on Williams's life might provide a useful introduction to his short stories.

Thomas Lanier Williams was born in Columbus, Mississippi, on 26 March 1911. His father was Cornelius Coffin Williams, a dashing, roguish salesman and a surprising choice for lovely young Edwina Estelle Dakin, who had her pick of eligible young men in Columbus. Edwina was the daughter of the local Episcopal minister and enjoyed the highest social, if not economic, standing in the community. The marriage was not made in heaven, and if the Williamses' domestic life was not quite hell, it was frequently unpleasant, increasingly so after the family moved to St. Louis in 1918.

Regardless of what the actual facts of the case may or may not have been, in later years Columbus came to seem a bucolic Eden to Williams, and St. Louis a cold, crowded, ugly blight where he was tormented by schoolmates because of his accent, shyness, and frailty. His beloved older sister, Rose, suffered along with him, but whereas Williams found some solace in his writing—he began writing stories and poems at least as early as junior high school—Rose's principal defense was to withdraw further and further into herself.

After graduating from high school, Williams escaped to the University of Missouri at Columbia, which he left after three years because of poor grades and inadequate funds. Back in St. Louis, Tennessee briefly attended Washington University and worked for a few months in the same shoe factory where his father was an executive, then enrolled at the University of Iowa. It was while he was at Iowa that Rose, who had been under psychiatric care off and on for years, accused her father of making sexual advances toward her, whereupon Edwina decided to allow a new procedure to be performed on her daughter: a prefrontal lobotomy. Williams never entirely forgave his mother for her hysterically hasty decision nor himself for being gone when the whole horrible event transpired. Rose thereafter became Williams's symbol for all that is beautiful and breakable in the world; ironically, she outlived him.

After graduating from Iowa in 1938, Williams spent the rest of his life in virtual transit. He traveled to Chicago, New Orleans, California,

4

New York, Italy and Sicily, and Florida, where he finally purchased a house in 1950, but he never spent more than a few months at a time there. His growing suspicions about himself—that he was homosexual—were confirmed again and again during his travels; a different sort of suspicion, or hope, that he was potentially a great writer, was confirmed in the mid-1940s with the success of his play *The Glass Menagerie* (1944).

The next decade and a half was a prolific period for Williams. His sexual appetite was surpassed only by his capacity for work. Among other awards, he won two Pulitzer Prizes for his plays during this period and published two collections of stories (and wrote half of the stories that later were to appear in a third collection, *The Knightly Quest* [1966], not to mention a novel and numerous poems). The "catastrophe of fame," and probably other, less understood, pressures, began to take their toll, however. Over the course of the years the quality, though not the quantity, of his writing declined and his reliance on drugs and alcohol increased. At a time when he most needed understanding and emotional support, he drove relatives, friends, and professional acquaintances away from him with his paranoia. He underwent psychotherapy—unsuccessfully. He converted to Catholicism—a ludicrous farce. He was finally hospitalized, much against his will; while there he suffered a series of heart attacks, and any salubrious effects of this drying out were short-lived. What is amazing, considering his life-style, is that he lived to be almost seventy-two. But when he choked to death on a medicine bottle-cap, alone in a hotel room in New York City on 24 February 1983, one might surmise that he did not much care.

What is it about his life that is important for us to remember? That Tennessee Williams was on intimate terms with loneliness, pain, violence, and death, but also passion, love, beauty; and that he was able to transform these intimacies, through the peculiar alchemy of his genius, into a voice and the voice into something resembling myth. Many more specific incidents and details from Williams's life appear in the stories, and where essential, these will be discussed. But more important is that beguiling interplay of voice and passion, recalled not always in tranquility, that marks the short fiction of Tennessee Williams.

"The Vengeance of Nitocris"

Tennessee Williams wrote at least twelve stories[2] before 1941, when his first fiction of unqualified merit began to appear. Of these dozen stories, only a third were published (prior to the posthumously published *Tennessee Williams: The Collected Stories* [1985]), and one of those appeared in a student publication at the University of Missouri and another in a pulp magazine *(Weird Tales)*. His pre-1941 fiction obviously is apprentice work, but it is interesting not simply because its weakness helps us measure his later success but because the seeds of that success are so evident in the early fiction.

Of his first published story, "The Vengeance of Nitocris" (1928 in *Weird Tales*), Williams has observed that "if you're well acquainted with my writings since then, I don't have to tell you that it set the keynote for most of the work that has followed."[3] Williams took the basic out-line of the story from Herodotus's *The Persian Wars*. Nitocris is the sister of a pharaoh who, for rebelling against his religious duties, is torn apart by a priest-led mob before his sister's eyes. Nitocris takes her revenge by constructing a temple on the Nile, inviting the priests, then trapping and drowning them in an underground vault. Realizing that she cannot long escape retribution, she fills a room with hot ashes and perishes therein.

Williams's later fiction is prefigured in this early story in a number of ways. Most obvious is the interrelationship of passion and violence— although the more mature Williams would hardly agree, one surmises, that "vengeance [is the] strongest of passions" (8). Prefigured too is the pattern of brother and sister aligned against a punishing world— although never again in Williams's work, fiction or drama, will the pair be so physically and emotionally fit to meet that challenge. In addition, the public dismemberment of the pharaoh is a scene that will be reen-acted more than once in Williams's stories (and most famously in the play *Suddenly Last Summer*).

Subtler parallels between apprentice and mature Williams are found in "The Vengeance of Nitocris," too. At sixteen, his age when the story was published, Williams probably had the barest, if any, inklings of his incipient homosexuality, yet already in the story we find that the most sensuous description is reserved for the brother. The sister is described in vague, general terms. "She was tall and magestically handsome as he [the pharaoh]. . . . She was the fair and well-loved Nitocris" (2). She may indeed have been as "magestically handsome" as her brother, but her brother's magesty evokes much more vivid imagery. "Superbly tall and muscular, his bare arms and limbs glittering like burnished copper in the light of the brilliant sun, his body erect and tense in his attitude of defiance, he looked indeed a mortal fit almost to challenge gods" (3). Some years later a more self-aware Williams will declare, "I cannot write any sort of story . . . unless there is at least one character in it for whom I have physical desire."[4] The pharaoh may be the first such example.

The most important technical feature of the story that also appears in later works is the distanced narrator, most evident in the beginning of the last section. "I would be content to end this story here if it were but a story. However, it is not merely a story" (11). In later fiction, Williams will use a distanced narrator to lend mundane characters and events a mythic scope, the grandeur of tragedy. Here, unfortunately, Williams's narrator is intrusive, almost comically insistent, with an effect the opposite of his intentions: events are robbed of their vigor and immediacy.

"The Vengeance of Nitocris," in fact, may well be the "keynote" for what follows, but it is also notable for how far it is from Williams's mature fiction. The prose is almost uniformly clichéd, strained, and dreadful. "Hushed were the streets of many peopled Thebes. Those few who passed through them moved with the shadowy fleetness of bats near dawn, and bent their faces from the sky as if fearful of seeing what in their fancies might be hovering there" (1). In other words, at this point in Williams's career he was writing just about the way one would expect a sixteen-year-old contributor to *Weird Tales* to write.

More important than the adolescent prose in the story is the adolescent worldview. Years later Williams remarked, "The one dominant theme in most of my writings, the most magnificent thing in all human nature, is valor—and endurance."[5] In "The Vengeance of Nitocris" the valor is preeminent; even in their violent deaths brother and sister are larger than life, superior to the vain and mundane machinations of mere mortals. Despite Williams's claim, in his later fiction, outright valor is difficult to find, and endurance often becomes something closer to hanging on, and not very long, against a pitiless and indomitable world.

"The Vengeance of Nitocris" is, then, a definitive example of an apprentice story, and it will do neither to exaggerate its "keynote" status nor to overlook therein the seeds of later success.

"A Lady's Beaded Bag," "Something by Tolstoi," and "Big Black: A Mississippi Idyll"

Williams's next three short stories, "A Lady's Beaded Bag," "Something by Tolstoi," and "Big Black: A Mississippi Idyll," were written between 1930 and 1932, during which time Williams was attending the University of Missouri at Columbia. "A Lady's Beaded Bag," in fact, was published in that school's literary magazine, the *Columns;* the latter two remained unpublished until the appearance of *Collected Stories.*

"A Lady's Beaded Bag" is the sort of effort one would expect from a college freshman who, up until that time, had exhibited no great potential. The story concerns a ragpicker who finds a beaded bag and, out of fright, returns it to the owner, only to have the owner show perfect indifference to the whole affair. "A Lady's Beaded Bag" is facile irony reminiscent of O. Henry or Maupassant at his worst. Because of its date of composition and its theme of downtrodden masses contrasted to the indifferent wealthy, the story could be seen as an early example of proletarian fiction—but that would be stretching a point indeed. More significantly, the ragpicker—"frantic as a small animal caught in a trap" (15)—is the first example in his fiction of the loner, the outsider, what Williams would later call the "fugitive." (Nitocris and her brother are outsiders, too, in a sense, but they are too haughty and powerful to qualify as genuine Williams fugitives, who are notable for their vulnerability as much as for their isolation.)

Whether "A Lady's Beaded Bag" marks an advance on "The Vengeance of Nitocris" is open to debate. Neither are interesting stories except insofar as they prefigure later, nobler achievements. We can say, however, that Williams's prose has improved somewhat in the later story. Indeed, an occasional sentence pulses with the wise sensuality of a much older writer. "He drew his finger over its [the purse's] soft, cool surface with the lightness of a cautious Don Juan caressing a woman of whom he is not sure" (14).

"Something by Tolstoi" is a more interesting story than "A Lady's Beaded Bag." In it a young bookseller marries an ambitious woman who soon leaves him to seek fame as an entertainer in Europe. Fifteen years later she returns to the bookstore but is not recognized, apparently, by her husband. She asks for a book and describes the plot, which is essentially the story of the couple's lives. "There is something familiar about the story," the husband muses. "I think I have read it somewhere. It seems to me that it is something by Tolstoi" (25). The story recalls O. Henry or Maugham more than Tolstoi, yet its ending is more thought-provoking, less facile than that of "A Lady's Beaded Bag." Here the husband's forgetfulness or indifference demands explanation. We might conclude that he is numbed by his wound—the wounded character a virtual archetype in Williams's fiction—or that certain situations are imbued with too much passion and pain to be faced honestly and directly—probably a combination of the two.

The story, alas, is more interesting in summary than in toto. It exhibits almost no compelling sense of place; the characterization on the whole is weak and shallow; at its best the narrative achieves a sort of mechanical slickness. Concerning its place in the development of Williams's short fiction, "Something by Tolstoi" is notable primarily for the author's attempt at a more complex narrative voice. Here the point of view is neither omniscient nor filtered through one of the two principals. Rather, the narrator is a young shop assistant, another of Williams's fugitives, as is clear in the opening lines. "I was dead tired and I felt myself a failure; the place looked like a quiet hole, in which a person could hide from a world which seemed all against him" (17). Using a secondary character as a narrator is an old strategy but, nevertheless, one that must be handled with some skill. Fitzgerald's choice of Nick Carraway as narrator of *The Great Gatsby* was a brilliant stroke, richly rewarded, but what does Williams gain by using his outsider as narrator? Nothing at all. It does show a young writer struggling to find out what he wants to say and how he wants to say it. If the struggle at this point is still largely a failure, that is to be expected. It is failure, after all, that defines an author's apprentice years.

"Big Black: A Mississippi Idyll" shows Williams still in search of a voice and subject matter—and coming closer to finding it. The title character is a member of a Mississippi road crew who labor in cruel heat and under the even crueler tyranny of the Irish boss. Big Black does not openly rebel, but periodically he rips open his shirt and bellows out a "savage" cry: "YOW-OW. YOW-OW-W-W" (27). Exactly what the enigmatic cry means, no one seems to know, but it invigorates Big Black's fellow workers. In the central scene, Big Black accidentally comes upon a white girl swimming in a river. He spies on her, then almost rapes her, stopping short when he realizes how bestial he has become. He dives into the river and swims away; the last scene finds him in Georgia, working on another road gang, periodically letting out his savage cry.

Once again, the story is riddled with clichés and generally shallow characterization, but we do not have to strain to find interesting elements. In between the clichés lurks some telling, violent imagery, a hint of the more mature Williams prose. The Irish boss, for instance, is "wet and fiery red as if he had just been dipped into a tub of blood"

(26). Big Black's hand during the near-rape scene seems to cover the white girl's face "like a hideous, huge black spider" (30). Moreover, the story exhibits a new and vivid sense of place—the American South. Any of Williams's previous stories could have been written by Maugham or O. Henry or Maupassant (in a weak moment), but not "Big Black." It is a *Mississippi* idyll, after all.

The "Idyll" part of the subtitle is also important. What still approaches shallowness also borders on something finer: a stylized quality invoking the mythic, the epic. The story is, or is intended to be, as "elemental, epical" as the cry that Big Black flings "like a challenge and like a prayer . . . at Life" (27). Moreover, the mythic quality is heightened by the first scene's ritualistic repetition at the end.

In "Big Black: A Mississippi Idyll" Williams does not yet have his considerable powers under control, but we can say that for the first time those powers are truly in evidence, and we receive a hint of at least one direction that those powers will take him.

"Accent of a Coming Foot"

Three years elapsed between the writing of "Big Black: A Mississippi Idyll" and the next selection in Williams's *Collected Stories*, "The Accent of a Coming Foot" (written in 1935). The years were significant for Williams in a number of ways. By then he had dropped out of the University of Missouri and had worked for a time in a St. Louis shoe factory, until suffering a breakdown of sorts (he called it a heart attack, a diagnosis not shared by his doctors). He continued to write poetry, and in 1935 coauthored a play that was performed by an amateur group in Memphis, where he stayed that summer with his grandparents. More important, perhaps, is what Williams had begun to realize about himself. His brief tenure at the shoe factory convinced him that he was not meant for success, or even employment, in more traditional lines of work. That he was destined to try to be a writer was already evident at the University of Missouri; and that this destiny would be in some ways a painful one—putting him beyond the pale in the eyes of his father, for one thing—was becoming equally evident. Two other realizations from this period are important. His homosexual tendencies were becoming clearer, disturbingly so, to him; equally disturbing was his sister Rose's deteriorating emotional condition, her inability to adapt to life's harsh realities.

It would be several years before Williams would directly employ homosexuality as subject matter for a short story, but his and Rose's inability to fit in with "normal" society is dramatized in "The Accent of a Coming Foot." Thus, "The Accent of a Coming Foot" is a watershed of sorts for Williams. For the first time he clearly employs his own experiences as substance for a short story, a phenomenon that will soon become the rule rather than the exception.

The personal experience is not directly recorded—this is fiction, after all, not reportage—but we do not have to delve very deeply to find Williams and Rose. The story concerns a young woman, Catharine, who returns to her home town after a year as a career girl in the city. She visits the Hamiltons: the mother, Mrs. Hamilton, her daughter, Cecilia, and son, Bud. Immediately the reader feels an undercurrent of tension. Bud has failed to meet Catharine at the train station, a lapse mother and sister find alarming but not totally unexpected. Bud, never quite the same as everyone else, has begun spending increasing amounts of time by himself. That he is spending this time primarily in writing does not seem sufficient justification to the Hamilton women.

Over the course of the story, a strange tension begins to grip Catharine as she waits for Bud to show up, and it is evident that the relationship between her and Bud has been a strong one. Exactly what that relationship was is not entirely clear, but sexual imagery predominates when she thinks of Bud. She expects to "see Bud's face peeking faun-like between the quivering shafts of green vine" (36). When she finally sees his shadow on the window, "she felt herself impaled like a butterfly upon the semi-darkness of the staircase" (40). When he opens the door and enters the hallway, however, Catharine stares down at him "like a haughty old dame," upon which "Bud bowed slightly from the waist as though this house were a bathroom which he had inadvertently entered at the wrong moment, finding Catharine there unclothed or in an unfortunate pose" (41). He backs out of the door and closes it, after which Catharine throws herself on a bed and weeps. The story ends.

What has happened? How does all of this pertain to Williams and Rose? The associations evoked by the story were powerful indeed for Williams, for he claimed to have suffered his first "heart attack" immediately after writing the story; the attack was brought on by "something too close to myself in the character of Bud and the tension of Catharine."[6] Most obviously, Williams and Bud are both writers. Bud had chosen his writing over the company of others and had been deemed "odd" for his choice. If Williams was not in fact the hermit in the attic, he was already living outside the sympathy and understand-

ing of his father and, to a degree, his mother. On a subtler level, however, Catharine also shares a great deal with Williams. Both had gone
out into the world, Catharine to a career in the city, Williams to the
University of Missouri. Both had returned to find things changed, for
the worse, and both have a hard time dealing with the situation. For
both, the overt changes are less important than their subconscious reactions to these changes. Catharine's inner tensions, more apparent to
the reader than to her, are reflected in the generally distasteful sexual
imagery. She cannot face, much less understand, her feelings for Bud.
Just so, the young Williams must have been having considerable difficulty coming to grips with his growing homosexual inclinations.[7]

If Williams is present in both Bud and Catharine, so too is Rose.
Rose's problem, Williams said over and over again, was rooted in sexual
frustration and hysteria. Catharine's emotional collapse at the end of
the story was frequently reenacted by Rose; only two years after this
story was written, Rose underwent a lobotomy. Moreover, Rose resembles Bud, whose name is the first of many "flower" names Williams
would employ in his fiction. Bud's sequestering himself to write is not
too dissimilar from Rose, who "often sat alone in the dark, waiting for
Edwina [her mother] knew not what."[8]

Two tendencies converge in "The Accent of a Coming Foot": Williams's tendency to divide himself, so to speak, between two or more
characters (i.e., both Catharine and Bud partake of their creator's char-
acteristics) and his tendency to blur, commingle the identities of himself and Rose. His tendency to discuss his and Rose's fates in the same
breath is seen in the following quotation: "I've had a great deal of
experience with madness; I have been locked up. My sister has been
institutionalized for most of her adult life. Both my sister and I need a
lot of taking care of."[9] Rose, after all, represents a fate that Tennessee
evaded only, perhaps, because he had his writing. Rose had nothing.

When we turn our attention to technique, we find that "The Accent
of a Coming Foot" represents a clear maturing. Williams follows the
modernist strategy (used by Joyce, Mansfield, Anderson, and others)
of investing seemingly trivial, everyday actions with great emotion and
significance. Nothing much *happens* in the story, after all, but what
does happen is dramatized in such a way as to lay bare the characters'
lives. The story's emotional intensity is conveyed in part through the
spare action and seemingly irrelevant dialogue, but primarily through
Williams's use of imagery. In "The Accent of a Coming Foot" we can
begin to see emerging the writer of great verbal power. In this story,

12

the potential is more evident than the accomplishment, exemplified in the telling but ultimately labored description of Catharine's hat.

> She talked for a while about her work in the city, but as she talked her head moved with such a nervous vivacity that the red cherries on her hat kept clinking brittlely together and she was unpleasantly reminded, for some reason, of a time in college when her coatsleeve had brushed against the arm of a human skeleton in the zoology lab: it had rattled like those cherries and she had glanced sharply up to see the death's-head staring straight in front of it with a fixed, grimly patient smile.
> (35–36)

"The Accent of a Coming Foot" is not, it must be admitted, altogether successful. Mrs. Hamilton and Cecilia are shallow and unconvincing characters, and as interesting as Catharine and Bud are, their conflict seems more *introduced* than fully realized. Yet the story is one more very large step down the road to maturity for its author.

"Twenty-seven Wagons Full of Cotton"

Also in 1935, Williams began a story, "Twenty-seven Wagons Full of Cotton," that was published the following year in the highly respected journal *Manuscript*. "Twenty-seven Wagons Full of Cotton" is the prototype for the one-act play of the same title, and the famous (or infamous) movie *Baby Doll* is also based in small part on the story. Obviously, then, "Twenty-seven Wagons Full of Cotton" was Williams's most successful story up until that time.

It is also more fully realized than any of his previous efforts. Although Williams does not attempt a very great deal in the story, what he aims to do he achieves with hardly a misstep. Therefore, the label "apprentice work" applies to "Twenty-seven Wagons Full of Cotton" only by a strict, and in this case arbitrary, chronological categorizing.

The story has an elemental simplicity. Twenty-seven wagons of cotton from a nearby syndicate farm have arrived at Jake Meighan's cotton gin, and while the daylong ginning is in progress, Mrs. Meighan entertains the syndicate man on the front porch of her home. The entertainment consists primarily of Mrs. Meighan's phlegmatic attempts to resist the syndicate man's advances. At the end she half retreats and half is forced into the house by the man, and we sense that her last words, "don't hurt me!" (48), preface something quite imminent and quite sordid.

All of Williams's previous stories smacked not only of apprentice fiction but also, at times, of juvenile fiction. With "Twenty-seven Wagons Full of Cotton," however, it will no longer do to be condescending about the young author's understanding of the world. The psychological truth of the story is supported by Williams's use of specific, accurate detail. "It was late in the afternoon. The gin stands were pumping and the pneumatic pipes still sucking. A fine lint of cotton was floating through the sunny air, across the tired gray road and the fields of copper-topped Johnson grass, grown nearly waist-high, and onto the porch where Mrs. Jake Meighan and her guest from the syndicate plantation were seated on the swing" (43).

The story's setting is not mere decoration. The characters' passions seem to arise naturally from the landscape—or perhaps one should say *unnaturally* from a landscape out of which life is unnaturally tortured into being by the cruel heat. Mrs. Meighan can barely move in the heat. She can hardly summon the energy to resist the syndicate man's advances, to object to his swatting her with the little whip. In fact, she almost *likes* the whip, when the man "didn't swing it too hard" (44). But the man swings it harder and harder, becoming more and more insistent, almost demonically so, we feel. "Hell's fire but you're big!" the man says (45).

Mrs. Meighan *is* big. "You're bigger'n the whole southern hemisphere" (46), the man says, twisting her wrist now. She no longer likes the game as much, tries, in her almost helpless way, to resist. She rises to go into the house, to make lemonade, she says. "I'll go in, too," the man says. "I'll squeeze the lemons" (48). She hesitates; he forces her into "the dark hall," where she begins crying, "a tremendous, sobbing Persephone" (48). Into the bedroom he propels her. "Oh, my God, it's so hot!" she moans. "Please, for God's sake . . . don't hurt me!" (48).

With the "tremendous sobbing Persephone" the story becomes not simply elemental but *mythically* elemental—but then it has been all along. Hence, the "Hell's fire"; "bigger'n the whole southern hemisphere"; "dark hall" of Hades; and the preternatural heat and pleas to God at the end. Mrs. Meighan is Persephone, forced by the demonic little man and the destructiveness of her own passions to enter the dark underworld of hot, adulterous lust, leaving behind a virtual wasteland broiling in the sun, with who knows what consequences.

Mrs. Meighan is not simply a grotesque Persephone, however; she is also Mrs. Meighan. Mythic parallels in fiction can be artificial and trite if not anchored to a vivid quotidian reality, and the latter is a greater and more difficult accomplishment than the former. Williams's great achievement in "Twenty-seven Wagons Full of Cotton" is the skillful wedding of the mythic and the quotidian. A hot Arkansas afternoon, for example, comes uncomfortably alive in the following description:

> Feeling a bit faint, she brushed the fuzz of cotton lint from her moist cheeks and leaned back in the swing which she kept lazily in motion with the lopsided heels of her white kid slippers. Her legs were bare. They had been shaved not so long ago but now they needed shaving again. The sweat trickled deviously between the stubbles of dark hair down the bulging calves and lumpy ankles and splashed into little pools underneath the swing. A swarm of flies was buzzing around her. The little man from the syndicate plantation kept brushing them off with his riding crop. Sometimes he struck her bare legs so smartly that it left a small red mark.
> (44)

In a letter to his grandparents,[10] Williams said that the story was supposed to be "humorous," a curious comment unless one notes that the young man (still living with his parents) was attempting to justify the story to his grandparents (and his grandfather a minister) after just describing to them how shocked his mother was by the tale. Rather than being humorous, "Twenty-seven Wagons Full of Cotton" shows that the young author already knew how powerful passion could be—and how destructive. Such would become one of his most frequent themes in fiction.

"Sand" and "Ten Minute Stop"

The years 1936 through 1940 were important ones in Tennessee Williams's life. Nineteen thirty-six witnessed his greatest literary success to that time, the publication of "Twenty-seven Wagons Full of Cotton" in *Manuscript*. In 1937, Williams entered the University of Iowa, from which he was graduated in 1938. Nineteen thirty-seven was also the year that Rose underwent a lobotomy. By 1939 Williams's pattern of restless travel was already established; more important, in that year he acquired a prestigious agent, Audrey Wood. Finally, by 1940 Williams was beginning to attract considerable attention as a playwright, with the opening of *Battle of Angels* in Boston.

Williams's *Collected Stories* includes six stories from the 1936–40 period. If "Big Black: A Mississippi Idyll," "The Accent of a Coming Foot," and "Twenty-seven Wagons Full of Cotton" seem to show an author assuming ever more confident command of his talents with each new effort, these next half-dozen stories remind us that writers reach learning plateaus, too, and even regress. None of the six stories in this period are as fully realized as "Twenty-seven Wagons Full of Cotton," although several are interesting in their own right and deserve some attention.

"Sand," Williams's next story, is not one of them. It is competently done, stylistically, but far too flat and static; the account of an old woman caring for her feeble husband, who suddenly remembers her in her youth, "Sand" is hackneyed and unenlivened by vivid imagery or evocative descriptive detail. Altogether, the story seems more "written" than profoundly felt by the author.

"Ten Minute Stop" is not entirely successful but is more interesting than "Sand." Were it not for the simple fact that Williams had not yet begun his wanderings in 1936, we could be forgiven for assuming that the story is directly autobiographical. At the beginning of the story, Luke is in Chicago, where he had come from Memphis in search of a job. (Williams also failed to find work in Chicago, coincidentally, but that was not until two years later, after graduating from Iowa, in 1938.) When he finds that his would-be employer is out of town, Luke takes the bus back toward Memphis. The ride and subsequent "ten minute stop" in Champaign are occasion for the disgruntled protagonist to consider his own condition and that of the downtrodden in general.

The theme of the downtrodden masses—1936 was not only the midst of the depression but also the height of the proletarian-fiction movement—is too vague to be very moving or thought-provoking. Although he occasionally attempted stories of a vaguely political nature, Williams was rarely very successful. Luke's personal plight is more interesting, however. He is another of Williams's fugitives, emotionally and, in this case, physically uprooted, homeless, alone. We never know precisely what awaits Luke in Memphis, but that seems to be part of the issue: he has no compelling reason to return to Memphis, no emotional reason to consider it a home. On the bus, "he didn't feel like himself. He felt as though the thread of his identity had snapped and he was moving on with nothing at all left behind him" (54). Over the course of the story he reaches the conclusion that the problem is not simply the loss of the job or the alienation many of us feel on buses (or in airports or subways); rather, his whole life is little more than a "ten minute stop in a strange town . . . just a ten minute stop! I get you, thought Luke. I don't belong. I'm not one of the actors" (58).

The story ends, for all thematic purposes, with that realization, but Williams drags it out by adding a rather pointless scene between Luke and some college boys. The scene is interesting only because the mob's brutal attack on Luke is an inchoate dismemberment scene, the first since the pharaoh's fate in "The Vengeance of Nitocris," but hardly the last in Williams's writing.

Williams knew no more where to go with his story, one surmises, than Luke knew where to go with his life. Still, we sense Williams struggling to expand his technical range. The "rootless" theme of the story is reflected in its structure, divided into increasingly short segments until, by the end, the last few segments (set off by line breaks) are no more than a brief paragraph or two in length. Concomitantly, Williams uses long lines—"And all that happened and was allowed to happen and the rich and poor alike lived and died, the fawning poets, the lewd and elegant lords, the prudish lascivious ladies, the diseased and ignorant multitudes—all these lived and died upon the earth and nothing was done about it" (58)—followed by bursts of short fragments: "Over and done long ago. Doesn't count anymore. New people to cover the earth these days. And the earth merrily reeling through space" (58). The fragmentation of narrative structure and grammar, paralleling the fragmentation of Luke's life, works better in theory than in practice. But it is all a part of a learning experience bringing Williams ever closer to genuine accomplishment.

"Gift of an Apple"

Much the same can be said for Williams's next story, "Gift of an Apple." Once again we find a young man on the road, this time hitchhiking from California to Lexington, Kentucky. The reason for the trip is never stated, underscoring the sense of rootlessness and alienation. Hitchhiking is easy enough in California, but once the young man reaches the vast emptiness of Arizona and New Mexico, it is harder and more dangerous. One must take his rides where he finds them, generally from drunks and "queers"—"all sons of bitches" (63). The central scene of the story occurs when the young man stops at an isolated house trailer to ask for something to eat. The fat woman who lives in the trailer will not share her dinner but does give him an apple. He eats it with great relish, and the woman gradually becomes sexually aroused by the young man but stops short of seducing him when she learns that he is the same age as her son. The young man leaves, and the story ends with him walking on down the road, regretting the missed meal but concluding that "maybe it was better that way, just having that taste in his mouth, the clean white taste of the apple" (69).

The full "meal" that the protagonist misses obviously includes the woman. The story is, indeed, filled with sexual resonances, not the least of which is the eating of the apple itself. "The hard red skin popped open, the sweet juice squirted out and his teeth sank into the firm white meat of the apple. It is like the act of love, he thought" (66). The hungry young man continually confuses images of sex and images of food. He remembers an earlier sexual encounter in an alley: " . . . all those cold wet smells. Potato peelings and cantaloupe rinds and damp coffee grounds. . . . And the nervous spasms and groanings. Not normal perhaps" (67).

Where does "normal" reside in the story? It is difficult for the reader to locate because this is a story about sex, and the young man's alienation is rooted in sexual disorientation. He is disgusted by having "to be groped all over to pay for your ride" (63) with the "queers." Memories of sex with the young girl are "sweet" but also vaguely disgusting, as the foul imagery pervading the recollection suggests. He is almost willing to trade sex with the obscenely fat woman for a meal, but more than just the age and size of the woman disturb him. She has hair on her chest, for one thing, making him think of the "hermaphrodite" at the sidewalk show (65), and this mannish woman, as the lust begins to burn within her, remarks, "You got nice skin like a girl's" (68). Little wonder that the young man feels relieved to get away at the end. His yearning to preserve that "clean white taste" of the apple (ancient symbol of sex, sin, and the Fall) represents a yearning for purity and normality—a normality that does not exist in harsh reality and, most especially, does not exist for an author becoming increasingly aware of his homosexuality.

The story works better in summary than in a close reading. The young man's alienation is not so convincingly dramatized as is Luke's in "Ten Minute Stop." At no point, in fact, is the conflict more than vaguely felt by the young man or the reader. One might conclude that the author has not yet squarely faced the issue of sexual disorientation himself; therefore, he is not yet able to dramatize vividly and passionately the conflict in his fiction. He is, however, coming closer.

"The Field of Blue Children"

"The Field of Blue Children" was the only one of the last six apprentice pieces to be published prior to Williams's *Collected Stories*, first in *Story* magazine (1939) and then in Williams's first collection, *One Arm and Other Stories* (1947).

"The Field of Blue Children" is Williams's most directly autobiographical story up until that date. The setting is obviously the University of Missouri, and the conflict concerns both sex and writing. The protagonist of the story is Myra, who one spring suddenly feels herself overcome with a "neurotic" restlessness that she can assuage only by writing poetry. She joins a poetry club and becomes infatuated with the poetry and the person of shy young Homer Stallcup. Eventually, they make love in the field of blue children, as Homer has described a flower-strewn field in a poem. Afterward, Myra becomes frightened at her impetuosity, returns Homer's poems, and marries a more normal beau. A few years later, she returns to the field and weeps, but then steadies herself: "now she had left the last of her troublesome youth behind her" (78).

"The Field of Blue Children" resembles "The Accent of a Coming Foot" in several ways. Here again we find a conflict between a young man and woman, and once again both represent aspects of their creator. Most obviously, the shy young poet Homer is the shy young writer Williams. Just as important, however, Myra's fear of her burgeoning sexuality and her desire for normality dramatize a time in Williams's life when he was beginning to awaken to his own abnormal sexual desires.[11] In both stories, significantly, the writer in the pair comes off the better. By trying to reject a frightening sexual urge, both Catharine in "The Accent of a Coming Foot" and Myra in "The Field of Blue Children" end by rejecting, Williams implies, a vital part of themselves: the spark of creativity. If Williams had not found refuge in his art, after all, he might have become another Rose—or a Myra, doomed to the sterility of a timorous normality.

"In Memory of an Aristocrat" and "The Dark Room"

The last two stories of Williams's apprenticeship, "In Memory of an Aristocrat" and "The Dark Room," were written in 1940. By then Williams had begun his life of travel, which took him, among other places, to New Orleans, the setting for "In Memory of an Aristocrat."

Williams loved New Orleans, and perhaps that fondness helps lend a lighter touch to the story of Carl, a young writer from the University of Missouri, and Irene, an artist and, in her own words, "whore." The story, in fact, displays some of the first touches of intentional humor in Williams's canon. The humor, unfortunately, helps vitiate the conflict, which occasionally seems a parody of the, by now standard, Williams theme of the sensitive artist in the hands of an indifferent, insensitive world.

Although "In Memory of an Aristocrat" manages to be entertaining even as it generally fails as a story, "The Dark Room" never quite manages to be even entertaining. The story concerns a social worker who pays a visit to Mrs. Lucca. Mrs. Lucca's daughter, Tina, is so distraught over an old beau's decision to marry someone else that she has stayed in her room, naked, in the dark, for six months. The social worker has seen a good deal of strange behavior, of course, but she is shocked to learn that Tina's one consolation is an occasional visit from the old beau. Yes, Tina remains in the nude during the "visit." The story dramatizes another standard Williams's theme: the power and destructiveness of passion. The story, unfortunately, is more shocking (if even that) than passionately felt and dramatized. The reader remains at a curious distance from the conflict, as if watching the reenactment of a perhaps true-life scene on a television monitor.

In both "In Memory of an Aristocrat" and "The Dark Room" Williams seems more concerned with technique than with a compelling dramatization of conflict. This is especially true in the latter story, which is composed almost entirely of dialogue. Strangely enough for a man who was America's greatest living playwright, Williams rarely loaded his stories with dialogue, if anything using less than most modern short story writers. In fact, an admittedly unsystematic browse through Williams's stories seems to show that the better efforts employ less dialogue than the inferior ones. It is difficult to account for this phenomenon except to observe that in the dialogue of even his great plays a very fine line often separates the sublime from the ridiculous.

(The easiest character to parody in American theater is Blanche Du-Bois—because she is so nearly a parody of herself.)

In contrast to the "pure" dialogue of "The Dark Room," in "In Memory of an Aristocrat" the dialogue is frequently rendered through indirect quotation, and even when characters are directly quoted, no quotation marks are used. Never again will Williams come so close to composing a story entirely in dialogue as he does in "The Dark Room," but he will use dialogue without quotation marks on a number of occasions and quite effectively, most frequently in his "memory" stories, when voices blend unobtrusively with other images from the past. The technique does not work so well in "In Memory of an Aristocrat," however, because it clashes with the near-burlesque tone.

Still, once more we have to conclude that the effort to find what works, even when the effort fails, is part of the learning process. By 1940 Williams was on the verge of applying, with dazzling success, all that he had learned.

Lessons of Apprenticeship

Just what had Williams learned during his apprenticeship? What aspects of his early writing can, in retrospect, he considered prototypical of his mature work?

These questions are difficult to answer with some writers because the apprentice years are for them largely a time of rejecting and abandoning that which does not work. Williams's thematic and technical inclinations were so strong from the beginning, however, that the roots of his mature work are plainly visible.

Williams never became a great innovator in the short story, but even in the apprentice period his willingness to try what were for him new techniques is evident, and his canon in general demonstrates a fairly wide variety of styles. In particular, he experiments with point of view, using the involved first-person narrator ("Ten Minute Stop"), the uninvolved first-person narrator ("Something by Tolstoi" and "In Memory of an Aristocrat"), and various degrees of omniscience. His experiments with dialogue have been noted; like the experiments with point of view, they are attempts to bring a certain immediacy to the action or, even more commonly, to distance the reader from the conflict, which, ideally, transpires in a sort of mythic nimbus ("Big Black: A Mississippi Idyll" and "Twenty-seven Wagons Full of Cotton"). "Big Black," "Twenty-seven Wagons Full of Cotton," and even "The

Accent of a Coming Foot" show Williams attempting to make setting a living presence in his stories. Taken together, the experiments with point of view, manipulation of dialogue, and importance of setting constitute the author's attempt to arrive at a certain texture of voice, which will become a hallmark of his fiction.

Two phenomena are noteworthy in regard to Williams's characters in the apprentice years. First, it is already apparent that he has a fondness for certain types of characters: the sensitive artist, the fugitive, the vulnerable soul buffeted by a harsh world, the person struggling, and generally failing, to come to terms with sex and passion. Second, these characters seem almost stock figures at times because they stand so much in service of a theme; they frequently seem representative, at times almost allegorical. When Williams is able to bring it all off, as he so frequently does in his mature period, his characters (and themes; we cannot separate them) have the power of myth. When he is less successful, the characters and stories seem shallow and lack immediacy.

Most obvious of all at this point in our discussion is Williams's willingness to employ autobiographical materials in his fiction. This tendency will grow ever stronger in his writing, and it is the secret of both his success and his weakness. Williams was never the indifferent artist sitting on the edge of the universe paring his fingernails—although he often tried to create a narrative voice that gave that impression. He created out of his passionate, personal concerns, and his best stories have the force of emotion deeply felt. However, his obsession with these passionate concerns led at times to staleness and, it could well be argued, eventually destroyed him as a man. Williams would have appreciated the irony. He lived it, after all.

Maturity (1941–52)

A writer's mature period is not always set off by some cataclysmic event or change in his life. More often, maturity is a culmination of sometimes barely perceived circumstances and trends established during the period of apprenticeship. So it is with Tennessee Williams. No major event occurred in 1941 that can be considered the cause or signal of his maturity. Perhaps the absence of a significant event, however, is as important as the presence of one might have been. By 1941 Williams had settled into a life spent largely in transit, from which pattern he would never vary. By 1941 his homosexuality was clearly, irreversibly established. Just as important, by the year that he turned thirty, he had spent half of his life as a writer and knew that thereafter he could do nothing other than be a writer. That he would be a great writer was still largely conjectural, but even his failures had convinced more than a few people in theatrical circles that his talents as a playwright were genuine and considerable; much the same, as we have seen, could be said of his potential as a short story writer.

"The Mysteries of the Joy Rio"

Williams's greatness as a playwright would not be clearly demonstrated for three more years—in 1944 with the opening of *The Glass Menagerie;* his writing of "The Mysteries of the Joy Rio" in 1941,[12] however, evinces masterly gifts and a unique vision. If the arrival of the mature Williams is signaled by anything other than the generally improved quality of his writing, it may be less an event than the fact that he is finally able to confront, and employ, a subject that he had only distantly approached in his apprentice fiction: homosexuality. Williams never did deal openly with homosexuality in his plays, much to the consternation of gay activists in the 1960s and later; he said that doing so would too narrowly restrict his audience. Beginning with "The Mysteries of the Joy Rio," however, homosexuality becomes a frequent and important theme in his short stories.

In bare summary, "The Mysteries of the Joy Rio" seems an uncommonly sordid tale. It concerns Pablo Gonzales, who at nineteen apprentices himself to the watch repairman Emiel Kroger. Pablo learns more than just the watch business from Emiel; the two live in homosexual compatibility until the older man dies, after which Pablo takes up the older man's practice of periodically visiting a local theater, the Joy Rio of the title. There Pablo, as Emiel before him, hides himself away in the dark balcony and, when he is lucky, takes brief and squalid comfort in the charms of some young man. Most of the time he is not so lucky and must take his comfort in masturbation. This pattern continues until one day, old and dying, Pablo surprises a young usher having sex with his girl (in the men's room). Enraged, the usher calls Pablo a "morphodite," and after a brief struggle Pablo escapes into the forbidden upper balcony where he dies in the arms of old Emiel, long dead.

Homosexuality, the thing itself, is too important to Williams and his work ever to be explained away as being merely representative or symbolic of anything. Still, homosexuality is but one very real manifestation of a broader phenomenon in Williams's work: the need for love and companionship and the difficulties of finding them in a world that grinds up the sensitive, the wounded, the fugitive. This is the theme of "The Mysteries of the Joy Rio," a story much more complex, tender, and moving than a bare outline of its plot would seem to indicate.

The story transpires against a tapestry of motifs and associations that lends a rich texture to events. The most obvious motif, at least early in the story, is time—Emiel and Pablo are watch repairmen, after all. At least two varieties of time operate in the story. One is the artificial, "witless" clock time to which Pablo, by the beginning of the story, already has become "indifferent" (99). Pablo's indifference to time has allowed him to "drift enviably apart from the regularities that rule most other lives" (100); while everybody else in the neighborhood "had an old alarm clock which had to be kept in condition to order their lives" (100), Pablo tells time "by light" (101).

Telling time by light may seem a more natural, hence healthier, mode than living by the artificiality of the clock, but such is not entirely the case. Time passes either way, for one thing, bringing inevitable age and death, and the wan light that suffuses "The Mysteries of the Joy Rio" is the somber, elegiac light of time running out. Of more immediate concern, Pablo's body clock is timed specifically to the afternoon light that reminds him when to go to the local cinema. This more natural time mode, then, directs Pablo to the setting for activities that are obscene and unnatural in the eyes of normal society. The Joy Rio itself is less a monument to entertainment than to time passing, aging, and, by the end of the story, death. It is an "old opera house" like those found in the "old world," with an interior of "faded gilt and incredibly old and abused red damask" (101).

The Joy Rio perpetuates another motif in the story: the mythic resonance. Earlier, Emiel is twice described as being "bewitched" by Pablo (99). The Joy Rio is bewitching in its own way. The "incredibly old" damask extends upward, who knows how far?—"at least three tiers and possibly five" (101). The top of the theater, above the forbidden ("roped off") upper galleries, is so "peculiarly dusky" that even the sharp-eyed Pablo "could not have made it out from below" (101). Moreover, "legends" surround the theater, which "make one more than usually aware of the short bloom and the long fading out of things" (103). This place of myth, and time, has a god, or rather an angel. "The angel of such a place is a fat silver angel of sixty-three years in a shiny dark-blue alpaca jacket, with short, fat fingers that leave a damp mark where they touch, that sweat and tremble as they caress between whispers, an angel of such a kind as would be kicked out of heaven and laughed out of hell and admitted to earth only by grace of its habitual shyness, its gift for making itself a counterfeit being, and the connivance of those that a quarter tip and an old yellow smile can corrupt" (103–4).

This pathetic, aging, damp-palmed, timorous yet conniving, and somehow slyly resilient angel is one of Williams's greatest creations, his Hamlet, his Leopold Bloom, and in one form or another he appears in almost all of Williams's stories, although his physical description will vary greatly. He is, here, the homosexual, but more important he is the fugitive, estranged from the society of men by his sexual preference or art or wounding shyness. Caught between heaven and hell, he is doomed to act out his drama on earth. The Joy Rio is Pablo's life, all there is. It is his "earthly heaven" (107), but also hell. He does find joy there, but it is a tortured joy, transient and cheaply purchased.

The angel, the aging homosexual, is also, of course, Pablo. The mythic resonances would be ephemeral or even hollow did they not emanate from a specific, human source. The story is moving and evocative because Pablo is credible and human. Early on he seems as banal and uncritical as his indifference to time might seem to suggest, but soon his role as the evocative center of the story clarifies and deepens as he ages before our eyes and becomes the lonely fugitive.

The process that the reader goes through in the story—of seeing past the banal surface of Pablo to the rich, tortured interior—closely mirrors the relationship of the homosexual and the world. Of necessity the homosexual must construct a false front, but the façade soon becomes a terrible burden. As old Emiel puts it, "The soul becomes intolerably burdened with lies that have to be told to the world in order to be permitted to live in the world, and that unless this burden is relieved by entire honesty with *some one* person, who is trusted and adored, the soul will finally collapse beneath its weight of falsity" (102). It is important to note that Emiel does not apply this description to the homosexual alone, but to the "soul"; similarly, in his biography of Williams, Donald Spoto summarizes the writer's belief that "if once you examine any honest nature . . . only the distortions necessary to survive a mad world—or dullness incarnate—will be so revealed."[13] Thus, not just the homosexual but "any honest nature" constructs distortions in order to survive, but then must break through his own distortions, share his true nature with *"some one* person," or suffocate under the weight of his mendacity and loneliness.

This process of sharing intimacies by breaking through façades is attempted by the homosexual and his lover; the fugitive and the *"some one* person" whom he finds, if he is very lucky; the reader and the protagonist; and most important of all, the author and his reader. Few processes of revelation are more intimate than that undergone by writer and reader—especially if that writer is Tennessee Williams. Sometimes this unburdening has the vitriolic directness of a Céline. Williams's variety is different, however, more complex. The mythic resonances distance events, as does the omniscient, sometimes intrusive, narrative voice. "And since it is not my intention to spin this story out any longer than its content seems to call for . . ." (105). One might surmise that the "content" is too painful to address at too close a narrative proximity—hence the myth, the intrusive voice, most of all the irony.

The irony is seen in the specifics, such as the seriocomic description of the "angel" cited above, as well as in the thematic irony, the catch-22 in which the homosexual—representing fugitives in general—finds himself trapped. He is isolated by his homosexuality from normal society—if such a thing exists—but has to live in the world anyway. In order to live in the world, he constructs a façade of lies. The lies become an intolerable burden, which must be relieved by *"some one* person." Relief in this specific case is homosexual relief, which starts the whole cycle all over again. Hence, the Joy Rio is at once Pablo's consolation and the symbol of the perversion that causes him to need consolation. It is his life and, at the end, his death.

In the middle of the story, Pablo recalls a bit of advice from Emiel, advice that could be said to be the bitter credo of the fugitive: "Sometimes you will find it and other times you won't find it and the times you don't find it are the times when you have got to be careful. Those are the times when you have got to remember that other times you *will* find it, not *this* time but the *next* time, or the time *after* that, and then you've got to be able to go home without it, yes, those times are the times when you have got to be able to go home without it, go home *alone* without it" (104).

At the very end of the story, as Pablo ascends into the mysterious upper regions of the Joy Rio, then falls into the arms of Emiel, into the arms of Death, the words come back to him again. This time the words are concluded by an observation from the omniscient narrator, perhaps still distant but no longer ironic, just heartbreakingly wistful: "The gentle advice went on, and as it went on, Mr. Gonzales drifted away from everything but the wise old voice in his ear, even at last from that, but not till he was entirely comforted by it" (109).

"Portrait of a Girl in Glass"

With the possible exception of "Twenty-seven Wagons Full of Cotton," all of the stories of Williams's apprenticeship period were found wanting for one reason or another. For even the best among them— "The Accent of a Coming Foot," "Gift of an Apple," "The Field of Blue Children"—praise was tempered with serious qualifications. No qualification is necessary for "The Mysteries of the Joy Rio," however. Because of its subject matter not every reader would enjoy it, but it is a masterful creation stylistically and thematically. Williams's unique genius is evinced in our feeling that only *he* could have written the story—just as only Joyce could have written his stories of Dublin, only Proust could have woven his peculiar tapestry of time; Faulkner was the sole owner and proprietor of Yoknapatapha. One story does not constitute a whole period in a writer's career, of course. "The Mysteries of the Joy Rio" is significant not only because it is itself an exemplary work of art but because it initiates a decade of accomplishment during which Williams wrote a score of stories, the best of which are as close as he ever came to greatness as a short story writer—and that was close indeed—and even the lesser of which are interesting, occasionally exhilarating.

Whether Williams's next story, "Portrait of a Girl in Glass," is one of his best or simply one of the merely good in this fertile decade is open to debate. The story's listing in the index to Spoto's biography of Williams is telling; after the title we find in parentheses, "(Williams story; basis of *The Glass Menagerie*)."[4] It is the inevitable fate of Williams's short fiction to play second fiddle to his plays, but that fate is an especially exasperating one when a story as fine in its own right as "Portrait of a Girl in Glass" becomes little more than a footnote to achievement in another genre.

"Portrait of a Girl in Glass" is a fine story, interesting apart from any association with its later incarnation. *The Glass Menagerie* takes its plot virtually unchanged from the story. The narrator (I shall call him Tom, although he is not named in the story) works in a shoe factory in St. Louis, stealing time from the drudgery to write poetry, returning home to his genteel but overbearing mother and pathologically shy sister, Laura. Laura is not lame in the story as she is in the play, but the other familiar particulars are present: the father has abandoned the family; Laura for some weeks has only pretended to go to business school; the mother wishes for "gentlemen callers" for the daughter; Tom brings one such caller home, only to find, just when things seem to be going well between Jim and Laura, that Jim has a steady girl.

As with the play, our attention is first drawn to Laura, the most famous of Williams's too sensitive, too vulnerable characters. If we hesitate to call her a fugitive, it is because that term seems to imply some movement, flight from the sharp daggers of the world that are always threatening to stab into the archetypal wound. Laura would be less haunted and haunting, perhaps, if she did flee, did do something, but, "she made no positive motion toward the world but stood at the edge of the water, so to speak, with feet that anticipated too much cold to move" (110). Her neurotic sensitivity is underscored by the image that Williams uses to describe what might otherwise seem an innocent and well-meaning gesture: her mother's enrolling Laura in the business course. In Tom's words, the mother "shoved her roughly forward" (110), and the damage is apparent and immediate.

Using *neurotic* and *pathological* in connection with Laura may be clinically correct, but such terms violate the spirit of the story. From Tom's perspective it is the world, not Laura, that is unnatural, pathologically cruel and unfair. In fact, descriptions of Laura are frequently invested with nature imagery, especially telling against the gritty setting of industrial St. Louis. Laura would fail the weekly typing speed drill, for instance, because the position of the keys would suddenly "fly from her mind like a bunch of startled birds" (110). Tom refers to her emotional withdrawal as closing "the petals of her mind" (112). When Jim comes to call, Laura finally appears, unsteady as a "tipsy crane of melancholy plumage" with "wing-like shoulders" (115). And her last name is the bucolic Wingfield—also the brother's and mother's name, of course, but Laura is the only character in the story to whom the name is directly applied.

The most significant nature image used in connection with Laura, however, is a good deal more ominous than those previously cited. Laura's room looks out over a cul-de-sac into which stray cats are chased by a "particularly vicious dirty white Chow" (111). What "appeared to be an avenue of escape," unfortunately for the cats, "was really a locked arena" where the cats meet their end, accompanied by "the screams and the snarls of killing" (111). "Death Valley" they nickname the cul-de-sac, and Laura keeps the shades drawn against the violent spectacle; "her days were spent almost in perpetual twilight" (111).

Her one solace is her eponymous menagerie, her collection of delicate, colorful, beautiful glass figures that line the walls of her room, casting winking light of varied hues into the perpetual twilight. The principal quality of the glass figures, perhaps, is their fragility. The symbolic fragility, the Death Valley at the end of the avenue of no escape beyond her own window on the world, and her own pathological shyness combine to doom Laura figuratively and literally.

The scene with Jim is less a thematic climax than a confirmation of the fate of the vulnerable in a cruel world. The last line of Laura's story, "She slipped quietly back to her room and closed the door" (119), has her where she had been all along. Laura is, indeed, a static character. We know no more about her by that last line than we knew after the first two or three paragraphs of the story. In fact, were the story Laura's alone, it would be pleasant enough, a delicate little thing, like one of Laura's glass figures—and probably no more enduring.

But the story is only partly Laura's. Laura is the focus, but in fiction we must pay careful attention to who is doing the focusing. Were the story only Laura's, it might well be told in time present by an omniscient narrator. But it is told in retrospect: "So time passed on till my sister was twenty-three" (114). A time present narration would heighten the sense of drama and immediacy. The retrospective narration, on the other hand, lends an air of wistfulness and tragic, but reflective, serenity to events, an air emanating not from Laura but from outside her, from Tom; and the reader is forced to consider the result of his reflection: that is, what Laura represents to him. This dual perspective—Tom's on Laura and ours on both of them—lends a richness to the story that would be missing if the story were Laura's alone.

Tom, indeed, is the first character mentioned and the one to whom our attention is first drawn: "Mine was an anomalous character, one that appeared to be slated for radical change or disaster" (110), he tells us in the second sentence of the story. Laura is introduced immediately thereafter, so the close conjunction of the "slated for radical change" and Laura's story seems to make the first dependent upon, or related to, the second. Tom and Laura are not so dissimilar as they may at first appear, after all. Both must put up with a domineering mother; both must resign themselves to an absent father (and it is Tom, not Laura, who speaks of this). Laura's room may look out on Death Valley, but Tom's room is also a "mousetrap" (112). His escape to the outside world—his job at the shoe factory—is only slightly more successful, and not much more ambitious, than Laura's brief tenure at the business school. Every evening when he returns from the factory, his nerves feel "worn rather thin from trying to ride two horses simultaneously in two opposite directions" (113). If Laura's social life is tragically limited, Tom's is not much better. He invited Jim to dinner because "he was the only one [at the factory] that I was on good terms with" (114). But how well does he know Jim? When Jim has finally left after the agonizing dinner scene, Mrs. Wingfield explodes, "I thought you called him your best friend down at the warehouse?" to which Tom responds, "Yes, but I didn't know he was going to be married!" Her concluding "How peculiar! . . . How very peculiar!" (118) must be shared by the reader.

Where does Tom go for solace after his lonely, tormented day at the factory? To Laura, of course. As weak and vulnerable as she is, still she is Tom's emotional support. She is, in fact, as beautiful, delicate, and fragile as one of her glass figures, and she bears about the same emotional and symbolic weight for Tom as the menagerie does for her. We know, without any question, that unless she gets out of her room at some point, her glass menagerie is going to come crashing down.[15] By the end of the story, unfortunately, we know that she will never leave her room.

Tom faces the same crisis. Unless he can overcome his almost neurotic attachment to and dependence on Laura, he is doomed, and the end of the story makes clear that this crisis—Tom's—is what the story has been about all along. The story ends just where it began: with our attention focused on Tom. He tells us that he lost his job in the factory: he "was fired for writing a poem on the lid of a shoe-box" (119). He left St. Louis and began to wander—and here the retrospective narration is most obvious. The wanderings were not always pleasant, we sense, but Tom matured: "I grew to be firm and sufficient" (119). The last paragraph tells us that five years have elapsed since Tom left home, and often he seems to have nearly forgotten Laura and his mother. "I had to forget it," he says. "I couldn't carry it with me" (119). Once in a while something causes him to remember, though: a certain radiance, a door opening, one of the tunes his "unknown father left [in the form of records that Laura loved to play] in the place he abandoned as faithlessly as I" (119). When this something intrudes, then he sees his sister's face, and—"the night is hers!" (119).

Earlier we noted that Laura bears about the same meaning for Tom that her menagerie does for her. We might extend that and say that the *story* bears the same proximate meaning for Tennessee Williams that Laura's menagerie does for her. This memory story could be seen as almost obsessively probing a wound, and this probing is something that Williams would be better off freeing himself from. But Tom is not Laura; he breaks away. And the story may be delicate and beautiful, but it contains a hard edge, the hardness that comes with looking directly and unblinkingly at the truth, awful as it is. (And it is awful, when one considers what happens to Rose [Laura] only a short time after events so dramatized.)

In autobiographical terms, one of the most interesting aspects of the story—interesting because Williams rarely addressed the issue so movingly elsewhere—is how Williams's father is in a sense redeemed by circumstances. A great deal of culpability and guilt is contained in that "abandoned as faithlessly as I" for both father and son.[16] But the point of the story is that the abandonment is necessary, else suffocation and madness reign.

"Portrait of a Girl in Glass," then, is another story—along with "Accent of a Coming Foot" and "The Field of Blue Children"—in which a male and female character share many qualities, but with the writer of the pair in a sense triumphing. The later story is immeasurably better than the two apprentice works, is almost a flawless story, strongly reminiscent of Chekhov—as is, for that matter, "The Mysteries of the Joy Rio." It would be a terrible shame if such a story came to be remembered—if at all—as a mere rough draft for a play, as exquisite as that play is.

"The Angel in the Alcove"

Like "Portrait of a Girl in Glass," Williams's next story, "The Angel in the Alcove," was later collected in *One Arm and Other Stories* (1948). Both were prototypes for later plays ("The Angel in the Alcove" for *Vieux Carre*), and both are memory stories in which the semiautobiographical narrator looks back at incidents that transpired at some point in the past. We have noted the distanced narrator often enough by now to claim it as characteristic of, though not universal in, Williams's short fiction. He seems to require a certain distance from his materials—especially the highly emotional conflicts dramatized in "Portrait of a Girl in Glass" and elsewhere.

"The Angel in the Alcove" shares as much in common with an apprentice story, "In Memory of an Aristocrat," as it does with "Portrait of a Girl in Glass." "In Memory of an Aristocrat," as its name announces, is another memory story, with the narrator at some distance in time—and also space, one would guess—from events. More important, the narrators of "In Memory of an Aristocrat" and "The Angel in the Alcove" are not so directly involved in the central action as is Tom in "Portrait of a Girl in Glass." For that reason, the latter story, even though narrated from a distance, is more impassioned and dramatic than the other two. In "The Angel in the Alcove" Williams also employs the technique found in "In Memory of an Aristocrat"—using dialogue without quotation marks—which heightens the memory quality of the story but perhaps causes it to fall short of the agonizing tensions of "Portrait of a Girl in Glass," where the more standard quotation marks are used. Finally, both "In Memory of an Aristocrat" and "The Angel in the Alcove" are set in New Orleans, with the narrator recalling a group of colorful, and sometimes nearly grotesque, characters but remaining largely aloof from the action himself.

On the other hand, it would be a mistake to say that the narrator does nothing at all in the story. The one scene in which he is directly involved, passive as he is throughout, is crucial not only for the story but also for Williams's entire canon; and by the end we may have decided, just as we did with "Portrait of a Girl in Glass," that the story was indeed the narrator's all along.

Although the story subsequently seems to focus on other characters, the opening lines imply that we are being introduced to a seminal event in the narrator's life: "Suspicion is the occupational disease of landladies and long association with them has left me with an obscure sense of guilt I will probably never be free of. The initial trauma in this category was inflicted by a landlady I had in the old French Quarter of New Orleans when I was barely twenty" (120). The first thing we notice about this passage is the Williams voice: easy, conversational, seductive. But also we sense the maturity—the narrator sounds much older than Williams's thirty-two years—and the almost epigrammatic wisdom—"Suspicion is the occupational disease of landladies"—suffusing the passage.

The dark cast to this serene opening, implied in the "obscure sense of guilt," is heightened in the portrayal of the landlady as the archetype (120) of suspicion. Soon she becomes almost mythically repulsive and repressive, lurking in the dark hallway of the boardinghouse like a black old spider waiting to catch a boarder trying to flee its trap: "You had to grope your way through it [the boardinghouse] with cautious revulsion, trailing your fingers along the damp, cracked plaster until you arrived at the door or the foot of the stairs. You never reached either without the old woman's challenge. Her ghostly figure would sit bolt upright on the rattling iron cot" (120).

Guilt comes easily to the narrator and other denizens of the allegorical boardinghouse—it is the world, of course. The guilt comes not so much from what they do—that could be corrected—but from what they are. Old Mrs. Wayne, for instance, is almost grotesque, but from where does her grotesquerie arise? From her almost obscene poverty. At the first scent of food, Mrs. Wayne will sidle through an unguarded door, beguile the rightful occupant with "horribly morbid or salacious stories" (121), then at the first opportunity help herself to a bit of food. Mrs. Wayne may strike the reader as grotesque, or at least pitiful, but she is memorable to the narrator because of "the spectacle of so much heroic vitality in so wasted a vessel" (121).

Mrs. Wayne is one of those characters who in time "disappear, the earth swallows them up, the walls absorb them like moisture" (121). As such, she is hardly more substantial than the next figure whom the narrator's memory lights upon, the angel of the title, a "tender and melancholy figure of an angel or some dim, elderly madonna" (122), who appeared to the narrator on especially melancholy days. The figure always vaguely reminded the narrator of his grandmother "during her sieges of illness when I used to go to her room and sit by her bed and want to say something or put my hand over hers but could not do either, knowing that if I did I would burst into tears that would trouble her more than her illness" (123).

The association of the grandmother with the angel is less significant than the shared sympathies and mutual self-sacrifice implied in the recollection. Although we might expect the recollection, and the angel, to be melancholy, they in fact *save* the narrator from melancholy.

"The Angel in the Alcove" may at first seem almost randomly organized, but Williams in fact moves easily and naturally from the mythically forbidding old landlady to the at once pathetic and heroic old Mrs. Wayne to yet a third old lady, the grandmother in the person of the angel. The next character introduced, a "tubercular young artist" (123), seems to indicate a break in the natural movement from old lady to old lady to old lady, but in fact the thematic unity is maintained and deepened. Like Mrs. Wayne, and the narrator, too, by implication, the artist is pathetic, wounded, a fugitive: "He lived in a world completely hostile to him, unrelentingly hostile, and no other being could enter the walls about him for more than the frantic moments desire drove him to" (124). In this case desire drives him to the narrator's room. "I want to, I want to," is all the artist can manage to say. The narrator makes no reply, but lies back "and let him do what he wanted until he was finished" (123).

The scene is important for being the first unvarnished homosexual scene in Williams's fiction (similar scenes being only implied in "The Mysteries of the Joy Rio"). The fact of homosexuality, however, is less important in the context of the story than what homosexuality represents: one fugitive (the narrator) sharing with another (the artist) all that he has to give, in an effort to assuage the pain of loneliness. In this sense the narrator's passivity in the scene is merely physical. Emotionally and even spiritually he is as actively engaged in another's torment as is the angel in the alcove—as is Christ on the cross.

The comparison to crucified Christ is not as farfetched as it may first sound. The narrator's decision to commit himself to the fugitive cause is not without its price. He himself becomes a fugitive, and the fate of the fugitive—homosexual, reclusive artist, poverty-stricken old woman—in the hands of an unyielding world, represented by the repressive landlady, is immediately apparent. In a marvelous dramatic scene, the artist confronts the landlady and complains of bedbugs in his bed. The landlady has obviously been waiting to "tell him off," and she does so with sadistic gusto. At the climax of her tirade, the artist becomes, in her words, what fugitives are to the world: less than human, less than insects. "You're the bugs that puts blood all over this linen! It's you, not bugs, that makes such a filthy mess at the Court of Two Parrots it's got to be scoured with lye ev'ry night! It's you, not bugs, that drives the customers off without paying their checks. The management's not disgusted with bugs, but with you!" (126).

The scene ends with the landlady throwing the artist and his belongings out into the rain, and the conjunction of rain and the artist's tuberculosis may indicate that the eviction will be not merely symbolically but quite literally fatal. The narrator shows his spiritual kinship with the artist by moving out, too, and he has wandered aimlessly ever since.

"The Angel in the Alcove" is a good example of the depth and emotional complexity with which the best of Williams's stories are invested. The depth of the narrator's feelings during the incident in which he aligned himself with the fugitive (homosexual) cause is obvious, but the complexity of those feelings warrants further comment. At no time in his life was Williams at ease with his homosexuality. Even the frankness with which he later addressed it—in *Memoirs*, for instance—is invested with more hysteria, masochism, and self-loathing than salubrious honesty. When the narrator of "The Angel in the Alcove" enlists, so to speak, in the fraternity of homosexual fugitives, he is joining a club whose principal qualification is loneliness and pain, an association which assures its members less solace than almost certain increased estrangement from "straight" society—hence increased loneliness and pain.

The narrator's submitting to the artist's advances is an affirmation of sorts, then, but it is an affirmation alloyed with regret and implied guilt. Guilt is evident when the narrator, immediately after permitting the sex act, looks toward the alcove to see what the angel's reaction is: "Yes, she was there. I wondered if she had witnessed the strange goings on and what her attitude was toward perversions of longing. But nothing gave any sign. . . . I felt that she had permitted the act to occur and had neither blamed nor approved, and so I went off to sleep" (124). It is important to remember that the angel has both sacred and secular connotations: sacred because she is, after all, an angel, but secular in that she reminds the narrator of his grandmother. Williams's maternal grandparents were important figures in his life, and grandmothers especially appear in a number of his stories. It was the few

35

months spent with his grandparents in Memphis that were his only real connection with Tennessee, of course, but much more important, the grandparents seemed to accept him on his own terms, not in spite of what he was, but because of what he was. He might have been an alien in his parents' house, but it was always "welcome home" at his grandparents' house.

It is both spiritually and personally significant, then, that the angel neither approves nor disapproves of the act but "permitted" it to occur. The angel figures prominently in events once more at the very end of the story. The narrator's departure from the boardinghouse follows closely the artist's, but a few days do pass between the two departures. During the interval, the angel fails to appear, "so I decided to give up my residence there" (127), the narrator recalls, the *so* indicating the close relationship between the angel's disappearance and the narrator's departure. The story ends, "I felt that the delicate old lady angel had tacitly warned me to leave, and that if I was ever visited by her again, it would be at another time in another place—which still haven't come" (127). Even at the end, the emotions and the angel itself are complex and ambiguous. The angel is still solicitous and protecting— a guardian angel—but she is also casting him out, forcing him on the fugitive road—a grandmotherly incarnation of the angel Gabriel, in other words, driving the fallen children from the garden. The narrator, thus, looks back fondly but with a sense of loss.

One final thematic impulse in "The Angel in the Alcove" deserves mention. All three fugitives are artists of one kind or another: the comsumptive young man is an artist, the narrator is a writer, and even old Mrs. Wayne is a beguiling storyteller. The first conclusion one is likely to reach—and a conclusion amply supported by other Williams stories—is that being an artist makes one a fugitive. This unhappy conclusion is softened by a more affirmative one, however. That is, art helps one to survive. We do not see the consumptive artist in the practice of his art, but Mrs. Wayne survives, literally, by her skill at spinning tales. Much the same could be said for the narrator—and Williams. The narrator travels manically from place to place but returns to New Orleans each time he is stunned by "some rather profound psychic wound, a loss or a failure" (123).

In returning to New Orleans he is attempting to return to the benevolent protection of the angel. The last line of the story tells us that he has never in his travels recovered the angel, but he does find her *in the story that he has told*, each time that he tells it. So does Williams. So do we. Indeed, the story, filled though it is with the painful and the grotesque, transpires in a mood that can only be described as elegiac, serene. The story, thus, inspires in us the same feeling that the angel inspires in the narrator and that, one would guess, storytelling inspired in Williams. Everything—friends, lovers, health, critical acclaim, self-respect—deserted Williams in the last two decades of his life, everything but the desire to write. When at last that left him, he died.

Variations on a Theme (1944–47)

Although not published until several years later, "The Mysteries of the Joy Rio," "Portrait of a Girl in Glass," and "The Angel in the Alcove" were all written in the 1941–43 period, during which time Williams's nomadic life had taken him to Hollywood for a mercifully brief and undistinguished stint as a scriptwriter. During this period, Williams also wrote and saw into production his most successful play until that time, *This Property Is Condemned*. Fertile for Williams as they in some ways were, the 1941–43 years might, in retrospect, seem a time of honing and shaping a potential that soon was to burst into a realization rarely equaled in American literature. The great shining forth began in 1944 with the production of *The Glass Menagerie* in Chicago. In only a little over a decade Williams won two Pulitzer Prizes and other major awards for his plays and wrote the bulk of his most interesting short fiction.

All this is not meant to suggest that each of his short stories over the next few years was an unqualified success. It is, however, one measure of his accomplishment to note how magnificent even a failure could be.

"Oriflamme."   The best example of a magnificent failure is Williams's next short story, "Oriflamme." In outline the story seems standard Williams fare. The protagonist, Anna, is another Rose figure, lonely, sexually repressed, too sensitive, a victim, a fugitive. That the Rose character's qualities are also uncomfortably close to the author's has been a familiar enough phenomenon in the past that we are not surprised to feel the same resonances here. Moreover, as is nearly always the case in Williams's stories, whatever feeble attempts the fugitive (Anna) makes to break out of the cycle of loneliness and repression end in failure.

The differences between "Oriflamme" and earlier (and later, for that matter) Williams stories are even more interesting than the similarities. Elsewhere, probably because the issues that he addresses are so painfully personal, Williams keeps a tight rein on his characters and his style. In "Oriflamme," however, Williams gives free rein to his creative and poetic powers. The story is set in St. Louis, but rather than being the grim quotidian presence it is in "Portrait of a Girl in Glass," for instance, St. Louis is more expressionistic than quotidian, at times no more than an extension of Anna's psychosis: "The air had been given those shots which the doctor suggested. The blue was not only vivid but energetic. And there was white, too, the sort of white that her hidden body was made of. A mass of bonny white cloud stood over the Moolah Temple. It suddenly made up its mind and started moving" (130).

Anna is the "bonny white cloud" who suddenly makes up her mind to move, and she is no more tied to the substantial world than is the fanciful cloud. She clothes her white body in a bright red dress, which she wears as a "flag" to signal her giving herself up to the "anarchy of the heart" (128). The story is splashed with evocative color, with red as its heart. Against the "clockwork . . . uniform" world (128), Anna decides, the "revolution begins in putting on bright colors" (129). Her walk through a very nearly surreal St. Louis takes her to the foot of a statue, a "fierce and compelling . . . menacing giant on horseback" (133), St. Louis himself.

Anna's revolution of the heart brings her no farther than to a dry fountain at the foot of fierce, phallic (he raises a sword) St. Louis. She sits down, overcome by an "avalanche of green" (133): decaying leaves in the bottom of the fountain, the park itself. A foam of blood crosses her lips, and the story ends in a burst of color. "The green of leaves, the scarlet ocean of blood, together they wash and break on the deathless blue. It makes a flag—but nobody understands it" (133).

"Oriflamme" is a strange wedding of impressionistic and expressionistic techniques, which reads a little like Katherine Mansfield revised by Franz Kafka. It is, in general, simply a bad story, obvious and heavyhanded early and willfully abstruse at the end. One would surmise that the final "but nobody understands it" includes the author.

Still, the story is an interesting failure and perhaps should be likened to a French symbolist poem rather than a traditional piece of fiction. Not only do the splashes of color recall Baudelaire, Rimbaud, and their colleagues, but the evocative and frequently untranslatable images might well be heartily applauded by the symbolists. Moreover, as is frequently the case with symbolist poems, "Oriflamme" verges simultaneously on the ludicrous and the sublime, exemplified by the following passage:

> It [the flag / dress] flashed, it flashed. It billowed against her fingers.
> Her body surged forward. A capital ship with cannon. Boom. On the
> far horizon. Boom. White smoke is holy. Nobody understands it. It
> goes on, on, without the world's understanding. Red is holy. No-
> body understands it. It goes on, on, without the world's understand-
> ing. Blue is holy. Blue goes on without the world's understanding.
> Flags are holy but nobody understands them. Flags go on without
> the world's understanding. Boom. Goes on without the world's un-
> derstanding. The heart can't wait. Revolts without understanding.
> Boom. Goes on. Without the world's understanding.
> (131)

The radical techniques used in "Oriflamme" do not arise from a willful desire to do things differently. Quite the contrary, the extremes of technique and emotion arise naturally from the givens of the story. In most other stories exploring variations on this same theme, the Rose character is balanced by another (the Tom character, let us say) who shares many of her problems, perhaps, but who is stronger, more able to stand the pain, more successful at reaching some accommodation with brute reality. In some cases these other stories are told by an omniscient narrator who is detached from the roiling passions that he describes. In other cases the Tom character is the narrator but is looking back over some distance in time, as in "Portrait of a Girl in Glass." In "Oriflamme," however, no distanced point of view intervenes between the reader and Anna, no more resilient Tom counterbalances her total vulnerability, and as a result all events reflect and are warped by her psychosis.

The result of this change in givens is not entirely successful, but "Oriflamme" does indicate that Williams refused to allow himself to become satisfied or complacent with a single fictive strategy. "Oriflamme" is a failure that helps confirm Williams's searching genius.

"The Vine."   Williams is less daring in his next story, "The Vine," and perhaps because of that more generally successful—the story won the Benjamin Franklin Magazine Award for Excellence in 1955. If, in "The Vine," he does not skirt perilously near the ludicrous as he occasionally does in "Oriflamme," neither does he test or extend himself very much.

Still, the story is hardly run-of-the-mill or without interest. Williams began the story in 1939, when he was twenty-eight years old, and finished it in 1944, when he was still only thirty-three. Not only was he a young man, at the peak of his physical and sexual powers, but he was on the verge of being an extraordinarily successful young man when "The Vine" was written. This circumstance makes all the more remarkable Williams's portrait of Donald, an aging, out-of-work actor who awakes one day to find that his wife has left him.

The story follows Donald through one miserable day as he tries with notable lack of success to adapt to life without Rachel. If he differs from the many Rose characters of earlier stories, it is not because he is any more able to bear up under the burdens of loneliness; rather, he differs from Rose in that we are less sympathetic with his plight—at least throughout the bulk of the story. "The Vine" is less tragic than generally comic in tone, and the omniscient narrator is less elegiacally than ironically distant from his subject. In the penultimate scene, in fact, when Donald brutally and foolishly tries to force himself upon a pointedly uninterested acquaintance, we feel that he fully deserves his reward: a stunning blow on the side of the head.

"The Vine" is a curiously cold story throughout much of its length because the protagonist is such an unsympathetic one. But the scene where Jane Austin boxes Donald's ears is merely the penultimate one. In the last scene Donald returns to his empty apartment, and the story changes considerably, just like the light in the room, which in his absence "had performed the circuit of a lifetime, from violence to exhaustion" (143). By the end of his day Donald's manic attempts to accommodate himself to life alone have ended in ludicrous failure, and he is alone with himself, his memories, and his dim prospects. He climbs into bed, curls into an "embryonic position [and] closed his teeth on a corner of the pillow, the one that was hers, and began to release his tears" (145).

His wife's return at that moment is not the sort of Hollywood resolution that it might in summary appear. She clasps him to her, and the story ends with Donald, a little child in the almost fleshless arms of the aging Rachel, reciting "the litany of his sorrows" (145)—an account of his humiliating day—as both weep for themselves and each other. Rather than a facile solution, Rachels's return and Donald's reaction to it emphasize how humiliating his day has been and how horrifying—

not ludicrous, not comic—life alone is. In the end we sympathize with Donald and perhaps even identity with him. Maybe, like Donald, we all are actors, vain, self-deluding, in need of comfort and companionship, fighting a losing battle against time.

"The Malediction."   Interesting as it occasionally is and award-winner though it may be, "The Vine" should not be considered one of Williams's major efforts. The prose is occasionally quite fine, but just as often flat and unimaginative: "Her cheekbones were awfully sharp. There was so little flesh on her arms, they were actually skinny" (145). Donald is less engagingly bemused early in the story than simply irritating; the end is more moving but verges on bathos: "'Oh, Rachel,' he sobbed, and she moaned, 'Donald, Donald!'" (145).

If we leave "Oriflamme" and "The Vine" with strong reservations about their success, Williams's next story, "The Malediction" is reassuring. It is strongly reminiscent of "The Mysteries of the Joy Rio," not only in tone, technique, and theme, but also in quality. "The Malediction" is, in short, one of Williams's most impressive efforts.

A rapid sketch of the plot seems to reveal a story with a strong political bent. Lucio, a rootless little man, wanders into a decaying factory town looking for a place to stay. He is taken in by a Mrs. Hutcheson, who looks to Lucio to provide the sort of "companionship" that her handicapped husband cannot. Mrs. Hutcheson arranges for Lucio to work at the local factory, and despite the soul-crushing dreariness of the work, things go well for a while. But then Lucio's brother, incarcerated on a robbery charge, is killed in a breakout attempt. Lucio loses his job when stockholders decide that a layoff would be most profitable. He gets drunk, gets thrown in jail, and returns to the rooming house to find that another has been given his room. At the end, clutching a stray cat that had taken up with him, Lucio walks into a river and, evidently, drowns himself.

Williams had shown a proletarian bent before in his fiction—especially in "Ten Minute Stop"—and would later also. Rarely does he make such a clear statement against fat-cat capitalists as he does in "The Malediction," however. Indeed, the eponymous curse is hurled at the capitalists in no uncertain terms: "'Lies, lies, lies, lies!' he [an old drunk] shouted. 'They've covered their bodies with lies and they won't stand washing! They want to be scabbed all over, they want no skin but the crust of their greediness on them! Okay, okay, let 'em have it! But let 'em have *more* and *more!* Maggots as well as lice! Yeah, pile th' friggin' dirt of their friggin' graveyard on 'em, shovel 'em under *deep*—till I can't *smell* 'em!'" (158).

It is a fairly reliable rule of thumb in dealing with Williams's work (stories *and* plays) that the more directly political a work becomes, the more it suffers. Williams was never a deeply intellectual writer—his genius was poetic, personal, and emotional—and he was rarely able to deal more than superficially with broad social and political issues. Such is the case with "The Malediction." The story does not suffer from its political impulse, however, because as central as that impulse appears in summary, it is never more than a sidelight in the story. Williams's superficial treatment of the political issue—and it is superficial—in this case is actually helpful because the issue never intrudes upon, but enriches, the context in which the more important theme operates. The true theme is the oldest in the Williams canon: the fate of the fugitive in a harsh world.

"The Malediction" abounds in fugitives. Lucio is the obvious example. He is "a panicky little man," a "lonely stranger, scared of his shadow and shocked by the sound of his footsteps," and his entrance into the "unknown town" (147) at the beginning is the archetypal fugitive situation. Even the cat that Lucio takes in is a fugitive, starving, lonely after being abandoned by a Russian, himself a fugitive who went west after he began to spit up blood. (The consumptive loner is a frequent enough character in Williams's fiction to be seen as archetypal.) Later, the laid-off workers comprise a band of fugitives of sorts; like other Williams fugitives their fate is all the more melancholy because it is inevitable. "Perhaps in the wombs of their mothers the veins that had fed them had sung in their ears this song: Thou shalt lose thy job, thou shalt be turned away from the wheels and the bread taken from thee!" (157).

One might almost conclude that everyone in "The Malediction" is a fugitive, with the exception of the factory stockholders, who are too sketchily rendered to be felt in human terms. The microcosm (individual as fugitive) become macrocosm (mankind as fugitive) impulse is supported by the story's rich mythic motif. The strange town that Lucio enters in the beginning is not so much a drab quotidian reality—as it probably would be in more truly proletarian fiction, for instance—as a supernaturally heightened world where "demon spirits that haunted a primitive world" creep along after Lucio, who "marches through watchful ranks of lesser deities with dark intentions" (147). Lucio "does not look at houses as much as they look at him" (147). Even the cat seems to become part of some ancient pattern from which Lucio cannot extricate himself. "I've sat here watching you for a long, long time!" (147) she seems to say.

The mythic motif does not merely serve as an opening tone-setter; it becomes increasingly important as the story progresses. Mrs. Hutcheson offers Lucio the Russian's room, "if you ain't superstitious about occupying [it]" (149). Lucio should be superstitious, because he is about to meet a character who smacks of the otherworldly, the supernatural. The old beggar who later utters the malediction stares with "eyes as enflamed as the cemetery-horizon before daybreak" and speaks in a "prophetic vein." *"Do you know who I am? . . . I'm God Almighty!"* (155). His claim is lent imagistic credence when he disappears into a "brightly lighted café" (155)—a nimbus of bright light indicating the presence of a god from the time of Homer onward. If the beggar is God, then even God is a fugitive: "God was perhaps," Lucio muses, ". . . a resident of this strangely devitiated city whose gray-brown houses were like the dried skins of locusts. God was, like Lucio, a lonely and bewildered man" (155).

If God can become a beggar, then perhaps a man can become God, and this is precisely what happens to Lucio at the end. The apotheosis is prepared for as the narrative eye pans back to a genuinely mythic distance and describes the coming of night in religious metaphor: "The earth averted this side of its face from the stinging slap of the sun and gradually gave it the other" (161). The religious resonances deepen as Lucio carries the cat into the cold water of a stream bordering a factory—sort of an industrial baptism, in other words. Briefly, the cat struggles in doubt: *"My God, My God, why hast Thou forsaken me?"* (161–62) she says, Lucio obviously the "Thou," hence the God. But then "the ecstacy passed" (162), and Lucio and the once-more faithful cat float away in the river. The story ends.

It could be argued, rather perversely, I think, that "The Malediction" presents some sort of religious vision, an affirmation of faith even in the face of martyrdom. The religious imagery is all there, as we have already noted. In this case, however, the religious imagery serves the tone of the story more than the theme. There is no point in the story, not one, where we associate genuine faith with one of the characters. Moreover, the tone of the story hardly supports an affirmative reading. Rather—in the absence of God—the religious motif is tragically ironic, underscoring Lucio's distance from charity, faith, and finally hope.

How abjectly pitiful Williams's characters are can be measured in what little they have to hold between themselves and the void and how desperately they cling to that little thing, whatever it may be. For Pablo in "The Mysteries of the Joy Rio" it was "a pleasure which was almost as unreal and basically unsatisfying as an embrace in a dream" (104). For Laura it was her so fragile glass collection. Donald clung like a vine to Rachel ("The Vine"), and because poor Anna had nothing at all to cling to, her world and story disintegrated into a fog of psychosis ("Oriflamme").

Years later, in commenting on the Russian icon that he kept by his bedside, Williams mused, "I don't suppose I would keep it there if I did not have some religious feeling"[17]—hardly a fervent avowal of faith. His 1969 "conversion" to Catholicism—inspired by drugs and a momentary desire to appease his brother, Dakin—is even less inspiring. Whatever Williams's beliefs may or may not have been, one thing is clear: his characters do not find God; if they are very lucky, they find each other, and then for only a short time, or they find art, which is a more faithful companion, but sometimes a cold one.

Lucio finds the cat, the cat, Lucio. They do not find God. The river upon which they float away is not a golden one, spiriting them off to heaven. It is a black one, taking them off to a cold, miserable death; it probably flows out of the brewery district of south St. Louis.

"The Important Thing." "The Malediction" dramatizes in the clearest, most moving terms the fate of the lonely. The mythic impulse does not complicate the theme so much as elevate the message to a universal, timeless level where we all become fugitives, swept away on the black tide of isolation. It is one of Williams's greatest stories, so grandly imposing that it makes otherwise quite competent and interesting efforts like its predecessor, "The Vine," and Williams's next story, "The Important Thing," seem rather shallow in contrast.

"The Important Thing" is hardly a bad story. It seems early on a rather smug satire on the intense but silly young college student; it gathers power, however, as an undercurrent of sex and violence grows toward a dramatic climax. The central figure, Flora, is another Rose character in name and personality. Her boyfriend, John, is more interesting; his rage during the attempted rape at the climax may stem less from frustrated desire than from the eruption of unacknowledged homosexuality. "The Important Thing" is finally, though, a reworking of themes Williams handled more imaginatively elsewhere, and is essentially an updated version of his apprentice story "The Field of Blue

Children." Indeed, were it placed with the apprentice pieces, where it seems more naturally to belong, "The Important Thing" would no doubt be seen as offering promise of great things for the young writer. In the midst of Williams's mature years, however, it is dwarfed by nobler accomplishments.

"One Arm."   One of those nobler accomplishments is Williams's next story, "One Arm." Like "The Mysteries of the Joy Rio," "Portrait of a Girl in Glass," "The Angel in the Alcove," "The Malediction," and only a very few later stories, "One Arm" shows the author in complete command of his powers as a short story writer.

"One Arm" is yet another variation on the theme of the fugitive, but this time with a harder edge. In a number of stories—and "The Malediction" comes perilously close to being a sterling example—the author's compassion for his characters is so great and so extravagantly evoked that compassion verges on pity; and pity is an unedifying emotional context for fiction. In "One Arm," though, we sense less pity than anger, and the fugitive, though he may indeed be a plaything in the hands of a cruel world, in this case can himself be cruel. He may not entirely deserve his fate, but he must share with the world at least part of the blame.

The telling difference between "The Malediction" and "One Arm" is that in the latter Williams returns to a subject that always evoked compassion and pity, but also anger and guilt in him: homosexuality. In this case the fugitive is Oliver Winemiller, a farm boy from Arkansas who joins the navy and becomes a boxing champion, only to lose an arm in a car wreck. All this is in the past. As the story opens, Oliver has settled less comfortably than mindlessly into the role of a male prostitute. The mythic evocations, so strong in "The Malediction," are present once again. Oliver "looked like a broken statue of Apollo, and he had also the coolness and impassivity of a stone figure" (175). His clothes are faded nearly white from washing, and they "held to his body as smooth as the clothes of sculpture" (175).

Oliver not only looks like a sculpture of a Greek god, but he is very nearly as cold as a slab of stone. He stares above the heads of passersby with indifference and conducts his business without passion or revulsion—without, indeed, thought. Only once does emotion stir him—in this case the emotion of rage—and neither he nor the narrator can explain exactly why one night after participating in a blue movie Oliver becomes enraged enough to bash in the skull of his client. He becomes a fugitive in the legal sense at this point but is inevitably captured, tried, found guilty, and sentenced to death. The bulk of the story transpires between Oliver's sentencing and execution.

"One Arm" is more interesting than some of Williams's less successful efforts that deal with the fate of the fugitive not only because in this case the fugitive is not so irredeemably pitiable but also because the fugitive is not our sole interest in the story. Oliver becomes more introspective during his incarceration, but even so his thoughts, and ours, turn increasingly toward those who would seem to be his victimizers: his "patrons," the wealthy men who buy his services. Gradually, we come to see that victim and victimizer are two sides of the same spiritual coin.

The imagery indicating Oliver's godlike physique is not merely decorative. Before his accident, Oliver was so fully integrated into the physical world, which was the only world of which he was aware, that the loss of the arm represents a separation of self from world, and ultimately self from self: "Oliver couldn't have put into words the psychic change which came with his mutilation. He knew that he had lost his right arm, but didn't consciously know that with it had gone the center of his being" (176). Centerless, he wanders indifferent to himself and others until "for no reason that was afterward sure to him" (177) he kills a man.

It is at this point, when Oliver's picture is published in the newspaper, that his clients enter the story as more than just faceless lechers. The mythic imagery does not subside but reenters in a new way, emanating from the clients. To them, Oliver "had stood as a planet among the moons of their longing, fixed in his orbit while they circled about him. Now he was caught somewhere, he had crashed into ruin" (178). A fallen angel Oliver may be, but the clients do not lose faith. Rather, they flood Oliver with letters recalling their experiences with him, "the few hours which they almost invariably pronounced to be the richest of their entire experience" (178). For them, Oliver has a certain indefinable quality, almost as if he were "the priest who listens without being visible to confessions of guilt. . . . To some he became the archetype of the Savior Upon The Cross who had taken upon himself the sins of their world to be washed and purified in his blood and passion" (179). With few options open to him, at this point Oliver makes just about the best choice a Williams character can make: he becomes a writer. He writes replies to his clients' letters. Oliver's letters are ungrammatical and awkward, filled with strained humor, false bravado, and fabricated recollections of intimacies shared; still, they spring from compassion and an intuitive grasp of his clients' plight. The letters are Oliver's finest moment.

The fact and effect of the letters cause us to reevaluate Oliver's mutilation, indeed, the meaning of his entire life. Psychologically and physically wounded characters abound in Williams's writing, perhaps the most famous examples being lame Laura from *The Glass Menagerie* and Brick Pollitt with his broken leg in *Cat on a Hot Tin Roof*. The wound generally represents acute sensitivity and vulnerability that prevent the character from living in the world as it is; the wound is the sore spot that the world seeks out, presses its horny nail into, and digs, digs. One would hesitate to claim the physical or symbolic loss of an arm as welcome, yet in this case the wound better enables Oliver to see the world and his place in it. His almost mythic, prelapsarian world of the physical was really an impossible world all along, and he could hardly be said to have lived in any meaningful sense until he became— not less vulnerable—but more sensitive to himself and those like him. In a certain sense, then, Oliver's wound is positive; we cannot say the same for Laura's or Brick's.

It is positive, however, only in a certain sense. At this point Williams could have ended his story in one of at least two interesting ways. He could have ended it with the epiphany of sorts that we have just described: the implied sharing of need and understanding between victim and victimizer. Or Williams, through his distanced narrator, could have trained a barrage of irony and bitterness against this epiphany, a strategy he would employ with ever greater frequency, unfortunately, in the last stages of his career. The former would imply a belief in a gentler, more ameliorable world than Williams has elsewhere vouched for. The latter would cheapen and, in a sense, make irrelevant Oliver's experience. Each possible ending would in its own way be facile and shallow.

Williams did not take the easy way out. He knew that a human being could be sensitive and brave and beautiful, and Oliver is all of these at one time or another, never more clearly than when he writes his letters. We admire him then even as we realize that all his bravery and beauty cannot hold back the world. "Coming prior to disaster," the narrator acknowledges of Oliver's newfound sense of communion with his former clients, "this change might have been a salvation. It might have offered a center for personal integration which the boy had not had since the mandala dream of the prize ring had gone with the arm"

(182). Ironically, Oliver might have been better off had he not traded his indifference for sensitivity. Indifference might have made his looming execution easier to take. Sensitivity makes it torture.

At this point, Williams introduces another major character, a young minister whose primary purpose seems to be to caution us against taking the religious imagery ("Communion," "confession," "Savior Upon The Cross," etc.) too seriously. The omniscient narrator makes us privy to the minister's dreams, and we know, better than he, that he has come to Oliver out of some repressed sexual urge, which is in sordid contrast to the "purer" need expressed honestly and almost sublimely by Oliver's clients. Oliver obviously senses this and offers himself with a slimy unctuousness designed to humiliate the minister. The scene is sadistic and masochistic, and beneath it swells the rage that earlier in the story drove Oliver to kill.

The story's cycle seems ready to repeat itself, but it does not. Williams will have none of Nietzsche's "eternal return." The next day Oliver is executed, leaving the emerging new cycle incomplete. "But death," as the narrator reminds us in the last line, "has never been much in the way of completion" (188).

"Desire and the Black Masseur."   Williams's next two stories, "The Interval" and "Tent Worms," represent a considerable falling off from the fictive heights reached in "One Arm" and other stories of the mature period. Both were written in 1945. "The Interval" remained unpublished, quite understandably so, until the *Collected Stories;* "Tent Worms" was finally published in 1980 in *Esquire,* adding lustre to neither *Esquire's* nor Williams's reputation.

Williams' next story,[18] "Desire and the Black Masseur," is one of his most famous. Donald Spoto calls it "a celebration of pain and the mute inevitability of self-sacrifice."[19] As such, it may be seen as a companion piece to "One Arm." Both show the destructiveness of passion and the interdependence of victim and victimizer.

The protagonist of the story is Anthony Burns, the "timidest kind of a person" (205), who works as a clerk in a wholesale company. Anthony is another of Williams's lonely souls; the depth of his loneliness is measured in how attracted he is to the characters in the movies that he frequents, the "figures who warmed him as if they were cuddled right next to him in the dark picture house" (205). Anthony's problem is not an absence but an excess of passion. His desire—the object of which is clear to us before it is to him—seems too large for his small person, and the result is that he feels "incomplete." Like desire, the concept of incompletion is less analyzed than simply pointed to by the omniscient narrator, yet it is obviously of great importance: "For the sins of the world are really only its partialities, its incompletions, and these are what sufferings must atone for" (206).

Like many of the stories in Williams's mature period, "Desire and the Black Masseur" is filled with religious language and imagery without being in any genuine sense religious. Anthony attempts to compensate for his incompletion through "the principle of atonement, the surrender of self to violent treatment by others with the idea of thereby clearing one's self of his guilt" (206). His instrument of atonement is the black masseur of the title, who is only too happy to administer ever more violent massages. Strangely enough, however, the punitive massages do not cleanse Anthony of desire so much as increase it to the point that he reaches a sexual climax. "So by surprise is a man's desire discovered" (209). Anthony's specific variety of "incompletion," then, is his homosexuality. His rituals of atonement (massages) grow more and more severe until, at the climax of the story, the masseur devours Anthony whole. Afterward, "quiet had returned and there was an air of completion" (211). The story ends with the black masseur moving on to another city and waiting with awful, godlike serenity for fate to bring him another victim. The last sentence tells us what we should have guessed—that we, all of us, are the next victim: "And meantime, slowly, with barely a thought of so doing, the earth's whole population twisted and writhed beneath the manipulation of night's black fingers and the white ones of day with skeletons splintered and flesh reduced to pulp, as out of this unlikely problem, the answer, perfection, was slowly evolved through torture" (212).

Whether or not "Desire and the Black Masseur" fully deserves its fame is open to debate. Its strengths and weaknesses arise from the same source: its single-minded pursuit of a theme. One gropes to recall a purer statement of the destructiveness of passion than that dramatized in this story. Every facet of the story serves the theme. Hence, the story becomes something like an expressionistic allegory. Anthony is a representative victim; he hardly stirs us with his individual plight. The black masseur never becomes more than an almost abstract agent of retribution; in fact, the brief attempts to invest him with a touch of depth—a racial motivation for his sadism (209)—are a shallow and unconvincing distraction. More important, the theme actually loses power through its single-mindedness. "One Arm" shows the destructiveness

49

of passion, too, for instance, but there the conclusion is less absolute, the relationship between victim and victimizer more complex and *human* and therefore more powerful and moving.

Still, there is no questioning the fact that "Desire and the Black Masseur" is a major effort, one of Williams's most important—if not best—stories; and it demonstrates that obsessed as the author apparently was with a single theme, he was always willing to experiment with approaches to that theme.

Williams's next two stories, "Something about Him" and "The Yellow Bird," are each interesting to an extent, but neither is fully enough realized to contribute measurably to Williams's reputation as a short story writer. "Something about Him" is a pleasant enough story, in which the heroine, Miss Rose (again!), almost gets her man, but it is too shallow and mechanical to be more than a good read of the *Mademoiselle* variety (in whose pages it was published in 1946). "The Yellow Bird" is much more interesting, a generally comic story in which the usual Williams's pattern of punishment for pleasure is reversed; here, those who give themselves up to desire get their just desserts, and those desserts are sweet. Still, the story is rambling and shallow, and although I dislike the practice of dismissing certain of Williams's stories as trial runs for the plays, in this case "The Yellow Bird" might best be remembered as the prototype for his great play *Summer and Smoke*.

Of the ten stories written in the main from 1944 through 1947 (some were begun earlier), three—"The Malediction," "One Arm," and "Desire and the Black Masseur"—unquestionably are major efforts. The remainder are uneven in quality, although all have something of interest about them. If the quality of the stories is uneven, each dramatizes in one way or another a theme that Williams had frequently addressed earlier, one that by now can be seen as his "figure in the carpet," if not his outright obsession: that is, the motif of the "fugitive kind," hounded by a cruel world and adrift between the Scylla and Charybdis of desire and loneliness. In all but "The Yellow Bird" the fugitive is too weak and wounded to stand much of a chance against the Furies pursuing him.

Although the stories are similar in theme, they show a fairly remarkable variety of styles, tones, settings, and narrative lines. This very variety has disturbing implications for Williams the short story writer, however. How much longer, if at all, one might well ask, could he continue to find new ways of approaching a subject that seems to have been pretty well picked clean? The answer to that question, found in his next half-dozen stories over the next three or four years, is the best indication of why Williams seems destined to be seen as occupying a secure place in the tradition of the American short story.

Fruition (1948–52)

No single event in 1948 signals a new phase in Williams's life; no single accomplishment or project indicates that Williams was entering a new phase of his career. Yet 1948 was an important year for Williams, as were the years 1948–52 in general. In 1948 he won the first of his Pulitzer Prizes, for *A Streetcar Named Desire*, confirming his status as America's most important playwright. More important for Williams personally, in 1947 he had met Frank Merlo, and by 1948 he had established, with Merlo, what was to be the deepest and most enduring romantic attachment of his life. In 1949 this semblance of something like stability in his personal life was strengthened when Williams purchased a home in Key West, the only permanent residence he was to establish in his adult life. (He never spent more than a few months at a time there, however.) In 1950 Williams received a Tony Award for *The Rose Tattoo*, and in 1952 he was elected—along with Newton Arvin, Eudora Welty, Louise Bogan, Jacques Barzun, and his good friend Carson McCullers—to a lifetime membership in the National Institute of Arts and Letters.

If there is such a thing as a golden age in a life marked by destructive passions, guilt, and paranoia, clearly the years 1948–52 represent such a time for Tennessee Williams. Although this period produced a similarly bright flowering in his short fiction, not every story written during that time is first-rate. "The Poet" and "Chronicle of a Demise," in fact, are dreadful stories, insipid allegories founded on no strong intellectual, emotional, or narrative basis; and "Rubio y Morena," though a fairly well-known story, is more interesting for its autobiographical elements than its intrinsic aesthetic worth. Still, four other stories— "The Night of the Iguana," "The Resemblance between a Violin Case and a Coffin," "Two on a Party," and "Three Players of a Summer Game"—are all major efforts and, along with a half-dozen stories from earlier in Williams's mature period, help establish his place in the tradition of the American short story.

"The Night of the Iguana."   Not entirely successful, "The Night of the Iguana" falls far short of the depth, breadth, and poetic power of the later play of the same name. Yet its protagonist is one of the most interesting women in Williams's short fiction, and her plight is at once representative of the typical Williams fugitive and an interesting departure from the stereotype. Altogether, despite some obvious failings, the story might well deserve inclusion among the author's major efforts.

In contrast to the plays with their Amanda Wingfields, Blanche DuBoises, Maggie Pollitts, Alma Tutwilers, and other remarkable women, Williams's short stories are dominated for the most part by men. With the possible exceptions of Mrs. Meighan from "Twenty-seven Wagons Full of Cotton" and Amanda from "Portrait of a Girl in Glass," Edith Jelkes, the protagonist of "The Night of the Iguana," is the first truly memorable female character in Williams's short fiction. Her story is at once familiar (to the Williams reader) and grotesque. As the story opens, it is the off-season at the pension in Acapulco where Edith stays. Her loneliness is exacerbated by the few tenants and the condescending, almost cruel treatment she receives at the hands of the staff. She is both fascinated and repulsed by the only two other tenants—homosexual, it is obvious to the reader, but not to her—who generally ignore her until she intrudes too brazenly upon their privacy. At the climax, one of the men, a successful writer, tries to rape her, but fails. The story ends with her once more in the loneliness of her hotel room.

As is the case with the best of Williams's stories, the relatively simple narrative line of "The Night of the Iguana" resonates with complex imagery, depth of characterization, and thematic impulses. One of the weaknesses of the story, in fact, comes from the feeling that the two men carry a good deal of emotional baggage around with them, but this baggage is never sufficiently opened for our inspection. (Williams solves the problem in the play by, among other things, the addition of the Reverand Shannon, a more fitting counterpart to Miss Jelkes.) Edith Jelkes is a much more satisfying creation, however. She had taught art at a private girls' school in Mississippi before suffering a "sort of nervous breakdown" and assuming a "life of refined vagrancy" (229)—before becoming the archetypal artist-fugitive, in other words.

Like many of Williams's women characters, Edith suffers from sexual anxiety, and Williams takes greater pains to explain the sources of this anxiety than is frequently the case in his short fiction. Edith, the omniscient narrator tells us, descended from a "Southern family of great but now moribund vitality whose latter generations had tended to split into two antithetical types, one in which the libido was pathologically distended and another in which it would seem to be all but dried up" (229). Edith was neither one nor the other type, "which made it all the more difficult for her to cultivate any interior poise" (229). As a spinster, she seems to have developed the pose of the dried-up type while possessing, but surprising, some of the "pathologically distended libido" of the other type. Her inner ambivalence is indicated by her dress. "The cloudy blond hair was never without its flower and the throat of her cool white dresses would be set off by some vivid brooch of esoteric design. She loved the dramatic contrast of hot and cold color, the splash of scarlet on snow, which was like a flag of her own unsettled components" (230).

Whether Williams's attempts to explain Edith's instability are interesting and illuminating or shallow and mechanical is a matter of opinion. Analysis was not Williams's strength; dramatization was, and the story becomes much more interesting when we see Edith in conflict with the pension staff and the two boarders. Edith is first drawn to the two writers by their studied indifference to her. Soon, she finds herself conducting a "seige" of the two, "even though the reason for it was still entirely obscure" (231). The two writers' indifference is "baffling" (230) only to Edith; we realize the transparently simple reason: they are lovers and as such will hardly find the attentions of a stodgy spinster welcome. And the reason for her "seige" is not "entirely obscure" to the reader either. The lonely are always drawn toward others, the sexually suppressed toward the openly passionate.

The lonely and suppressed only *approach* others, however. Communion is rare; that is why they are lonely, after all. At the same time that Edith is drawn to the two, she finds reasons to hold them at a distance, chief among them the young writer's (Mike's) habit of completely disrobing on the beach. Her protests are met with ridicule by the pension staff. It is soon after this that the iguana makes its appearance in the story. The iguana has been captured by the *Patrona's* son and tied beneath her window, where it is alternately tormented by local children and left to starve and suffer from thirst. The iguana's plight is an obvious (perhaps too obvious) metaphor for Edith's own, and she is so upset by the iguana's suffering that she complains to the writers. That the writers represent sexual abandon, as opposed to the repression of Edith, is implied in Williams's sensual description of them as they lie languidly in their hammocks fresh from a round of rum-cocas. "The liquid had spilt over their faces, bare throats and chests, giving them an oily lustre, and about their hammocks was hanging a cloud of moist and heavy sweetness" (235).

The writers are not quite so interested in the iguana's plight as is Edith, and they are less than overjoyed when she decides to abandon her room above the creature and take one next to them. When she overhears them making fun of her, she confronts them. Not only is the nature of her complaint similar to her earlier one about the iguana, but so is the language; hence, in case there was ever any doubt, we now see quite clearly that Edith and the iguana are, metaphorically, one.

At this point the story becomes even more interesting, at the same time that its weaknesses become more apparent. Williams's thematically and philosophically ambitious aim becomes more evident as religious and mythic imagery proliferate. Edith looks at one point "like a female Saint on the rack" (236). "I am not in any condition to talk about God" (237), the writer comments in the same scene; but later, in response to Edith's asking if he does not need someone's help, he replies, "The help of God! . . . Failing that, I have to depend on myself" (243). Soon, the religious imagery becomes mixed with the mythic. An approaching storm looms "like a giant bird lunging up and down on its terrestrial quarry, a bird with immense white wings and beak of godlike fury" (244). Watching the approaching storm, Edith, the narrator surmises, may have been "on the verge of divining more about God than a mortal ought to" (244); but at this point the older writer attempts to rape Edith. The mythic allusions surrounding the storm are intensified as the writer assumes the role of the swan (Zeus) and Edith, Leda. "He thrust at her like the bird of blind white fury. . . . A sobbing sound in his throat, he collapsed against her. She felt a wing-like throbbing against her belly" (244).

The throbbing is in reality the writer, unable to consummate the rape, ejaculating against her. She flees back to her apartment to find the iguana now freed from his rope. "Was it an act of God that effected this deliverance?" (245), the narrator asks. Or was it Mike, jealous of the attentions being paid to another by his lover and wanting to insure that Edith will have no excuse not to return to her room? "No matter," (245), concludes the narrator. Truly, it does not matter greatly. Mythic or mundane, Edith's experience has been dramatic—and not entirely bad. At the very end she lies in her room, alone once more, and touches the spot of semen on her belly. Her fingers "expected to draw back with revulsion but were not so affected. They touched it curiously and even pityingly and did not draw back for awhile. *Ah, life,* she thought to herself and was about to smile at the originality of this thought when darkness lapped over the outward gaze of her mind" (245).

The ending is brilliant and thought-provoking, surely one of Williams's best. Edith's experience has been horrifying and humiliating, but also quite clearly enriching. She will look back on it, it is possible, as the best experience of her life. (But the darkness closing in at the very end reminds us that Williams will not take the easy way out; there are no easy affirmations; everything has its price.)

Were the rest of the story as good as its ending, "The Night of the Iguana" would indeed be one of Williams's greatest. The climactic scene, however, is at once the most provocative and the most disappointing. The older writer, for instance, is a character potentially as interesting as Edith. In fact, they are a good deal alike; both, in their own ways, are iguanas. But his motivations are only hinted at, his character too thinly sketched. Similarly, the religious and mythic motifs show Williams striving for a more ambitious statement, but it all never comes together, and too often striving seems straining.

Obviously, at some point Williams decided that fuller development of his themes and characters would wait for the play.

"The Resemblance between a Violin Case and a Coffin." This story is another "Rose" story and an obvious companion piece to "Portrait of a Girl in Glass." This time a surname is not offered, but the fictional family is even closer to Williams's actual one than were the Wingfields. "Grand" (Williams's nickname for Edwina's mother) is mentioned by name, as is Tom and an aunt Isabel (the story is dedicated to Isabel Sevier Williams). More significant, the central incident in the story—a disastrous violin recital—closely resembles an actual one experienced by Rose.[20] "The Resemblance between a Violin Case and a Coffin" is set somewhat earlier in the process of Rose's emotional decline than is "Portrait of a Girl in Glass." Here, the family has not yet moved to the dismal "northern city," St. Louis; Rose (she is not named in the story) has just entered puberty, is still attempting to function in the everyday world, and still holds out some hopes for romance. By the end of the story, these hopes and attempts to function are dashed, which may help explain why she is a generally static character in "Portrait of a Girl in Glass."

At least in reference to Rose, "The Resemblance between a Violin Case and a Coffin" dramatizes a failed rite of passage. Tom sets the stage for the conflict by telling us in the story's opening lines that Rose "seemed to have gone on a journey while she remained in sight" (270). The journey is from childhood to adolescence. More specifically, Rose has just begun to menstruate, and the experience alarms her. Such a reaction is not entirely unique, of course, but it does help prepare us for her subsequent problems with the harsher aspects of reality, especially those involving sex. For awhile we hold out some faint hope for Rose. She seems to have some small talent for and interest in the violin, and she is girlishly fond of a fellow music student, Richard Miles, who is not totally indifferent to her. As the date of her violin recital approaches, however, Rose's debilitating shyness waxes. Her small command of the violin begins to erode, and her music teacher withdraws her solo number from the recital, leaving her to perform a duet with Richard. Rose freezes on stage and cannot finish the number, and Richard helps her off the stage and comforts her.

Richard's kindness and gallantry might, in the hands of another author, have led to the sort of resolution favored in formula romances. But Tom's description of Rose as she rides home from the recital hints at her spinster fate. "When I looked at her I noticed that her shoulders were too narrow and her mouth a little too wide for real beauty, and that her recent habit of hunching made her seem a little bit like an old lady being imitated by a child" (281). Richard fades out of their lives, and soon afterward the family moves to the "northern city," where a couple of years later they hear that Richard has died of pneumonia.

The reading experience of "The Resemblance between a Violin Case and a Coffin" is similar to that of "Portrait of a Girl in Glass." In both stories our attention is initially focused on Rose (or Laura); in both, however, we soon sense that the girl is too pathetic, doomed from the outset, to bear a great deal of narrative weight. We realize that Tom has been the important character all along.

Early in the story, when the onset of Rose's menstruation is introduced, Tom's reactions—"I was baffled and a little disgusted" (271)—are as important as Rose's. Moreover, if her anxiety over menstruation foreshadows sexual instability, much the same can be said of Tom's reactions. While his old play-partner stays in her room and contemplates her womanhood, Tom hides in the house, afraid to go out alone where the "rougher boys" torment him with "obscene questions that would embarrass me to the point of nausea" (271).

That these "obscene questions" might be directed toward any deviant sexual tendencies that the boys might suspect in Tom is pure conjecture at this point in the story. However, Tom's latent homosexuality soon becomes evident. "My sister's obsession with Richard may have been even more intense than mine" (275), Tom says, exposing himself far more than Rose. "She had fallen in love. As always, I followed suit" (275). Young boys often develop a love for older boys that is better termed hero worship, of course, but Tom makes it quite clear that the flesh was very much a part of his interest in Richard. Through the thin cloth of Richard's shirt "could be seen the fair skin of his shoulders. And for the first time, prematurely, I was aware of skin as an attraction. A thing that might be desirable to touch" (276). So enthralled is Tom with Richard's "dreadful beauty" (276) that his interest in his sister wanes. A "devout little mystic of carnality" (278) though he may be, this homosexual interest at the expense of a more childish attachment to his sister represents a movement toward maturity.

Rose's rite of passage is truncated, therefore, ending in the sort of hopeless isolation that we see in "Portrait of a Girl in Glass," while Tom's passage toward adulthood is more successfully navigated. His recognition of his homosexual tendency is only part of that passage, however. Tom must find some means of dealing with all the problems—homosexuality, an indifferent father, a pathetic sister for whom he cares *too* much—that have the potential to force him into the same sort of withdrawal from life that Rose is in the process of undergoing. His means of coping is through writing.

"The Resemblance between a Violin Case and a Coffin" is narrated from a distance in time in that serenely elegiac voice that we see so often in Williams's short stories, especially those dealing with a Rose character. The stance is not simply that of a brother, but that of a *writer*. "And it was then, about that time, that I began to find life unsatisfactory as an explanation of itself and was forced to adopt the method of the artist of not explaining but putting the blocks together in some other way that seems more significant to him. Which is a rather fancy way of saying I started writing" (274). Tom is interested in Rose's fate, of course, and in his own growing self-awareness, but he is also interested in the technical progress of his story. At times this awareness of the process of writing approaches the self-referential intensity of the phenomenon—associated with though not isolated to postmodernism—called metafiction. A passage such as the following would more often be associated with avant-garde writers such as Samuel Beckett and John Barth than with Williams: "I now feel some anxiety that this story will seem to be losing itself like a path that has climbed a hill and then lost itself in an overgrowth of brambles. For I have now told you all but one of the things that stand out very clearly, and yet I have not approached any sort of conclusion. However indefinite, there is always some point which serves that need of remembrances *and stories*" (my italics; 278–79).

Such metafictive passages may be seen as distractions in the story, but they are organic distractions. Were the story Rose's alone, then the passages would be inappropriate, better deleted. The story's ultimate theme, however, concerns how Tom survived his rite of passage and managed to survive not simply the fate of his sister but his sister herself. He escaped her through homosexuality (Richard, as Tom tells us, is a substitute for Rose) and writing. Hence, the metafictive passages, like the story itself, are healthy distractions from the morbid obsession with Rose.

Were he alive today, no doubt Tennessee Williams would object bitterly to this reading. It seems clear that Rose may have been the best and most beautiful thing in Williams's life; she was also the most dangerous, however. She was stasis, failure, and pathetic capitulation; and Williams's homosexuality, enormous appetite for writing, even his apparently self-destructive reliance on drugs, may have been, at least in part, attempts not only to live with the guilt over Rose but to distance himself from her, avoid her trap.

"Portrait of a Girl in Glass" and "The Resemblance between a Violin Case and a Coffin," then, as much as they may seem tragedies from a certain perspective, are also affirmations. Tom may look back in guilt and sorrow, but he also looks back in relief. He escaped.

"Two on a Party."   Only Tennessee Williams could have written such a story as "Two on a Party," and quite possibly only Tennessee Williams would have wanted to. "Two on a Party" is close to being a bad story; it is also close to being the most original and distinctive short story in Williams's canon. It seems frequently carelessly written and self-indulgent, but those same passages may well be the story's strength, evidence of a strange sort of courage and certainly of honesty. It is a story in which the narrator—call him Williams—gives himself up to superficiality and dangerous hedonism, hence risks trivializing himself and his experience; at the same time, in this intensely autobiographical story Williams comes nearer to accepting and affirming what he is than at any other time in his short-fiction career. As is always the case in Williams's best stories, however, the situation is too complex for a simple summary.

The plot itself could not be much simpler. Billy and Cora meet in a Broadway bar that both are "cruising"—looking for young men to pick up. After an initial misunderstanding, the two become friendly and decide that they can be more successful in their ventures by working as a team. Eventually they make their way to Florida where, in a not very climactic climax, Billy is beaten by a young hitchhiker, whose violent attentions Cora manages to divert by seducing the young man as Billy slumps bleeding against the wall. The story ends the next morning as Billy and Cora prepare to set out once more; the party goes on.

It is one of the ironies of this story that to explore the significant we must be careful not to look past the superficial (the party); it would be a regrettable misreading to see the party as allegorical (a variation on the "ship of fools" motif, perhaps) or to see the party as a mere veneer beneath which are more important subtleties. The subtleties are there, and significant, but significant too is the party in and of itself. The party is the principals' chosen life, after all. The narrator presents this life in enough specific detail that we can understand something of the quotidian mechanics of "cruising," and he also pans back so that life-as-party is seen from a more general perspective. "Usually or almost always it's only a breakdown that takes you off a party. A party is like a fast-moving train—you can't jump off it, it thunders past the stations you might get off at, very few people have the courage to leap from a thing that is moving that fast, they have to stay with it no matter where it takes them. It only stops when it crashes, the ticker wears out, a blood vessel bursts, the liver or kidneys quit working" (293).

One might guess from a rapid plot summary that the dangers and inanity of the party might be the point of the story, which would then become a sort of cautionary tale. But such is not the case. Cora is based closely on Williams's good friend Marion Black Vacarro; whether Billy is based on the poet Oliver Evans, as Gore Vidal claims,[21] or is a "clear surrogate for Williams," as Donald Spoto believes,[22] is an interesting but not crucial question. What is much more important is that the *narrator* speaks for Williams, and although the narrator is fully aware of the dangers of the party, he celebrates and embraces it.

One of the most interesting features of "Two on a Party" is the tone of the story, transmitted through the narrative voice. Here the voice is not serenely elegiac and nostalgic, or mythically detached, as is the case in the majority of Williams's major stories; rather, it is alternately condescending toward its subject and delighting in it, manic, jocular, playful, and *participatory*. As the excitement of the party intensifies, for instance, the narrator becomes so caught up in the scene that he loses his powers of description. "The night was a great warm comfortable meeting of people, it shone, it radiated, it had the effect of a dozen big chandeliers, oh, it was great, it was grand, you simply couldn't describe it, you got the colored lights going, and there it all was, the final pattern of it and the original pattern, all put together, made to fit exactly, no, there were simply no words good enough to describe it" (286).

The no-words-can-describe-it strategy is loudly lamented by most critics, and rightfully so. Indeed, the narrative voice sometimes becomes irritatingly cute and silly—"Then comes the badman into the picture!" (295)—the more so as the story progresses. This false, forced, condescending tone can be highly irritating, but we should not overlook the possibility that it arises naturally and appropriately from the characters and the conflict. The party *is* superficial, false (in one sense at least), and forced. But no one is more aware of it than the characters and the narrator, and blending the sublime and the ridiculous, in tone, shows the honest awareness and acceptance of all of it. Learning to accept the party is learning to accept oneself. Billy and Cora accept themselves for what they are in the story, and perhaps in writing it Tennessee, for a moment, accepted himself, too. "Why do *we* do it?" (my italics; 301), the narrator asks after Cora debases herself with the hitchhiker. "We're lonely people. I guess it's simple as that" (301), he answers himself.

The opposite side of the manic, careless glibness of the party, then, is loneliness. It is always there, for all of us, perhaps, as the repeated "we" implies. Billy and Cora join the party to escape loneliness and aging—" . . . the one great terrible, worst of all enemies, which is the fork-tailed, cloven-hoofed, pitchfork-bearing devil of Time!" (292); and if staying on the party exposes one to danger and degradation, the alternative is not very attractive: Rose.

In fact, however, there may be no alternative. The party may well be all there is, and choosing deliberately to ride it out, with an acceptance of the responsibilities entailed, may be an existential triumph. The story does not end with Billy's beating and Cora's degradation— not the first time for either, after all. That night they lie together, "hands clasping and no questions asked" (301). Afterward they can face each other in full knowledge, with something like pride, in fact. "In the morning, a sense of being together no matter what comes, and the knowledge of not having struck nor lied nor stolen" (302). And then?—"Off they go" (302), still on the party, Cora waking Billy in the morning "gently" with a cup of coffee, spilling a little perhaps. "Oh, honey, excuse me, ha ha!" (302).

"Three Players of a Summer Game."   Like "The Night of the Iguana," "Three Players of a Summer Game" was later reincarnated as one of Williams's great plays—*Cat on a Hot Tin Roof*. The stories are similar in that each offers a rich suggestiveness and provocative characters, all of which receive more profound treatment in the subsequent plays.

"Three Players of a Summer Game" profits more from comparison to "Two on a Party," however. The two were written during the same general period (1951–52), were both eventually published on Williams's second collection, *Hard Candy: A Book of Stories* (1954), and could well be seen as companion pieces, or perhaps bookends—encompassing the same general material but pointing in opposite directions. As bad as things get in "Two on a Party," the story ultimately affirms a resiliency in the human spirit and a self-awareness and self-acceptance among the "fugitive kind" rarely found elsewhere in Williams's canon. "Three Players of a Summer Game" ends with the human body and spirit humiliated, broken, enslaved.

The three players of the title, comprising a love triangle of sorts, are the formerly great athlete Brick Pollitt, his wife Margaret, and a woman with whom Brick has an affair, Isabel Grey. Margaret is the alter ego of Cora from "Two on a Party." Billy gets along so well with Cora because, among other things, "she had none of that desire to manage and dominate which is a typically American perversion of the female nature" (289). Margaret, on the other hand, seems to feed on Brick like a vampire, or like an insect devouring its host from within.

> Two sections of an hourglass could not drain and fill more evenly
> than Brick and Margaret changed places after he took to drink. It
> was as though she had her lips fastened to some invisible wound in
> his body through which drained out of him and flowed into her the
> assurance and vitality that he had owned before marriage. Margaret
> Pollitt lost her pale, feminine prettiness and assumed in its place

something more impressive—a firm and rough-textured sort of hand-
someness that came out of her indefinite chrysalis as mysteriously
as one of those metamorphoses that occur in insect life.
(306)

The reason for this parasitic relationship is never adequately explained in the story, nor is the cause of Brick's fall from a position of
almost godlike grace and beauty. Brick's problem is never clarified in
the play either, which in the eyes of the critics is either a major flaw or
an intriguing ambiguity. It is definitely a flaw in the story. The one
explanation the narrator, and Brick himself, give is his alcoholism, a
debilitating problem not to be glossed over lightly,[23] to be sure, but too
mundane, too specific, a problem to support the grand, mythic tone
and scope of the story.

As much as any story since Williams's apprenticeship, "Three Players of a Summer Game" seems eviscerated by its flaws and weaknesses, and not small ones at that. Margaret, after the big buildup seen
in the preceding quotation, virtually disappears from the story until the
very end; she is more a principle than a character. Brick's romance with
Isabel Grey is a frail thing, doomed from the start and lacking interest
and drama. (Williams drops the romance in the play.) The narrator—a
young boy who plays with Isabel's daughter, Mary Louise—tells us of
"a summer that was the last one of my childhood" (304), causing us to
suspect that the story will be a rite of passage of the complexity and
emotional depth of "Portrait of a Girl in Glass" or "The Resemblance
between a Violin Case and a Coffin." It is not. The relationship with
Mary Louise goes nowhere; what the narrator learned, if anything,
about life, love, art, or himself can only be guessed. And the story
contains too little evidence to allow us to make an educated guess.
Moreover, the game of the title, croquet, is not simply an ambiguous
metaphor for the character's condition, but a hopelessly inadequate
one; and the more Brick and the narrator focus on croquet, the more
irrelevant it seems.

In what may seem a laughable contradiction, considering the foregoing catalog of sins, I must say that few stories offer more compelling
testimony to Williams's greatness as a writer than "Three Players of a
Summer Game." Only an author of formidable talents could fail in so
many important ways and still produce a story that is intriguing to the
point of mesmerizing and, as I believe history will prove, memorable.
Williams's talents are most evident in his prose, which rises above the

flawed plot, characterization, and theme. In Williams's prose the horrible can at once be ghastly and beautiful, hence Dr. Grey's brain tumor. "An awful flower grew in his brain like a fierce geranium that shattered its pot" (307). Elsewhere Williams's descriptions combine the concrete and the abstract in a compelling and original way: the Pollitt's house "is of Victorian design carried to an extreme of improvisation, an almost grotesque pile of galleries and turrets and cupolas and eaves, all freshly painted white, so white and so fresh that it has the blue-white glitter of a block of ice in the sun. The house is like a new resolution not yet tainted by any defection from it" (303).

Primarily, however, the strength and chief interest of "Three Players of a Summer Game" is in the narrative voice. It is the voice that we come back to again and again in Williams's fiction, but not always is it the same voice. We perhaps first think of the elegiac nostalgia infusing Tom's voice in "Portrait of a Girl in Glass" and "The Resemblance between a Violin Case and a Coffin." Just as memorable, however, is the mythically detached, though ultimately sympathetic, voice in "The Mysteries of the Joy Rio," "The Malediction," "One Arm," and others. Less characteristic of Williams's fiction—at least at this point in his career—but just as interesting is the flip, condescending, ironic, but finally moving voice of "Two on a Party."

In "Three Players of a Summer Game" the voice is at once nostalgic and mythically distant, but in a different way than in Williams's previous stories. In "The Resemblance between a Violin Case and a Coffin" we noted that Tom has escaped what we might call the "Rose syndrome" and is able to deal with his guilt and *use* it by becoming a writer; indeed, he proves that by calling our attention to his writing the story that we are reading. The same general phenomenon occurs in "Three Players of a Summer Game," but the narrator is at an even greater, formal distance, so that the characters, plot, and so forth become abstractions, mere building materials of the story. Indeed, the game of the title seems to be less croquet than art, hence the formal, abstract opening lines. "Croquet is a summer game that seems, in a curious way, to be composed of images the way that a painter's abstraction of summer or one of its games would be built of them. The delicate wire wickets set in a lawn of smooth emerald that flickers fierily at some points and rests under violet shadow in others . . . the formal design of those wickets and poles upon the croquet lawn—all of these are like a painter's abstraction of a summer and a game played in it" (303).

The figures in Williams's story are more like *players,* imagined and set in motion by the consciously conjuring artist, than characters who pulse with virtual life. "And I associate the summer game with players coming out of this house, out of the mysteries of a walled place, with the buoyant air of persons just released from a suffocating enclosure, as if they had spent the fierce day bound in a closet, were breathing freely at last in fresh atmosphere and able to move without hindrance" (303). The metaphor of characters as players (perhaps playthings would be an even better image) becomes more explicit in a later passage. "There they all are, the bits and pieces, the images, the apparently incongruous paraphernalia of a summer that was the last one of my childhood, and now I take them out of the oblong box and arrange them once more in the formal design on the lawn" (304). Finally, players come to take on the more specific connotations of *dramatis personae,* and one might speculate that Williams was already beginning to envision his short story as a play. Of Brick: "Then the lawn would become a great stage on which he performed all the immemorial antics of the clown" (316–17). And to the neighbors, "the widow and her daugher and Mr. Brick Pollitt had been three players in a sensational drama which had shocked and angered them for two acts but which now, as it approached a conclusion, was declining into unintentional farce, which they could laugh at" (319).

In a certain sense, "Three Players of a Summer Game" reminds one of the Argentine Julio Cortázar's great short story "Blow-up," in which a writer, never leaving his room, imagines and reimagines, arranges and rearranges his materials. Williams's story is less technically daring than Cortázar's, yet taken in the context of Williams's other stories in his mature period, it gives evidence of just how innovative Williams could be, how varied his methods were in dramatizing a fairly small number of subjects and themes. One recalls Faulkner calling *The Sound and the Fury* his greatest novel because it was his greatest (most ambitious) failure. "Three Players of a Summer Game" is not Williams's greatest story, too flawed to be a great one at all, but it is a magnificently interesting failure and far more interesting than perfect stories by more timid writers.

It is a fitting conclusion to Williams's most fertile period as a short story writer.

Decline (1953–83)

After the bright flowering of the 1940s and the early 1950s, Tennessee Williams's talents began to fail him. If we cannot with total confidence account for the decline, certain factors are probably significant. For one thing, alcohol abuse had begun to have adverse effects on Williams as early as 1951. In 1955, Williams's grandfather died. He had lived with him off and on for years, and the grandfather was one of the few persons, apparently, who accepted and loved Williams for who he was. His father died only two years later, in 1957. If the relationship between father and son was less symbiotic than between grandfather and grandson, it was at least as important. Cornelius frequently comes off as the villain in Williams's writings, but Williams shared a good many traits with his father. Indeed, it is possible that only the Cornelius in him enabled Williams to escape Rose's fate—which is the point of "Portrait of a Girl in Glass," after all. Closer to Williams in many ways than his father was his lover Frank Merlo, the chief steadying influence in Williams's life after the "catastrophe of fame"; but this relationship began to sour by 1961. The 1960's were a haze of growing alcohol and drug dependency for Williams. Psychiatric help (as early as 1957, shortly after his father's death), forced hospitalization, and the ministrations of family, friends, and lovers all eased the pain only briefly and occasionally. The last two decades of Tennessee Williams's life were, in general, a horror.

Still, such a chronicle of woe does not necessarily account for Williams's artistic decline. His life was hardly serene at any point, and, in fact, his great works had often evolved from painful personal circumstances. Writers, and scholars attempting to account for turns in their careers, often fail to acknowledge a simple fact of existence: everything—trees, rocks, clouds, men—has a youth, maturity, and decline to oblivion. For every Henry James who hones and deepens his craft over the course of a long career, there are a dozen writers—very fine ones—who enjoy a bright decade or so and then either repeat themselves or noticeably decline. It may simply be that Williams had had his decade, and we should be grateful for that. It was a glorious decade, after all.

As conjectural as the causes of Tennessee Williams's decline may be, the fact of the decline can hardly be disputed. Williams's *Collected Stories* includes twenty titles written in the dozen years of his mature period, but only seventeen in the over three decades that remained of his life. Whether a falling off of quality paralleled the diminishing quantity is a matter of opinion, of course. However, in my opinion not a single story from these later years is the equal of "The Mysteries of the Joy Rio," "One Arm," "Two on a Party," or a half-dozen others from the mature period.

Still, all of this does not necessarily signify that Williams's later stories are without merit and unworthy of attention. Williams possessed the sort of genius that might fail him in certain ways but that even in failure could rarely be uninteresting. Moreover, although one aspect of his decline is the inability to find new themes and subjects, he continued to search for new effects, new ways to say what he had, regrettably, said too often already.

The prospect of an aging writer—lonely, paranoid, drug-ridden— still struggling to create something worthy of his reader is at once tragic and triumphant.

"The Coming of Something to Widow Holly."   The first story[24] of these later years, "The Coming of Something to the Widow Holly," is a perfect example of how Williams's short fiction managed to remain interesting, while falling short of the stature achieved by his major efforts in his mature years.

The story concerns Isabel Holly, widow and owner of a New Orleans rooming house. Her only boarders, an old bachelor and two spinsters, are constantly at one another's throats, and the widow's furniture and glassware are used as ammunition in their confrontations. About the only distractions the widow has from this bellicose trio are the creditors who besiege her house, hurling threats and obscenities at the cantankerous old bachelor, who refuses to pay even for his coffin.

The widow's life, in short, is wretched. One day a business card mysteriously appears under her door advertising the services of A. Rose, Metaphysician. She visits the old man, complaining that something seems to be missing from her life. And what is missing? A. Rose asks. "An explanation," she replies. "Oh—an explanation!" he returns. "Not many people ask for *that* anymore" (328). Neither the widow nor the reader finds A. Rose's explanation very illuminating or convincing. The widow Holly is, he assures her, "the first of your kind and character ever to be transplanted to this earth from a certain star in another universe!" (329). We have a much better explanation. Old, weary, vulnerable, alone—the widow is hardly unique; she is one more in the long succession of fugitives who populate Williams's fiction.

Not long after this visit to A. Rose, the widow sees one of the boarders, Miss Domingo, slip into the house with a box of explosives. The widow manages to escape just before an explosion wrecks the house. Miraculously, no one is killed, but the place is a shambles, and soon the three boarders make preparations to leave. At what seems the bleakest moment of the widow's life, A. Rose returns from Florida, where he had gone "to stay young forever" (332), transformed into Christopher D. Cosmos, a godlike young man who magically repairs the house and encourages her to burn all remnants of her past life. The story ends with the widow ascending to the bedroom where Christopher waits in bed, a smell of roasting apples suffusing the house, "an odor of celebration in the season of Advent" (334).

The last image of the story, conjuring the season of Advent, recalls the title, the *coming* (advent) of something. The religious implications of Advent, Christopher D. Cosmos's name (Christ of the cosmos), his note to her from Florida ("Dear Love to all my enemies" [332]), and other images and associations might lead one to conclude that what has come to the widow is Christ, salvation. If this is indeed what Williams intended the reader to take from his story—a possibility I find difficult to accept—then the story is unconvincing on an emotional, intellectual, and certainly spiritual level. We never for a moment believe in the thinly allegorical Christopher D. Cosmos or his earlier incarnation, A. Rose, whose name (arose) prepares us for the Christ figure. Indeed, the reader familiar with the Williams's canon will likely dismiss the Christian connotations of A. Rose in favor of a much more enduring archetype in Williams's stories: his sister Rose. The solution that Rose offers is not heaven but capitulation, psychotic withdrawal, death. What comes to the widow at the end is surely just that: withdrawal to her cold, empty bedroom, followed by death. In this reading, the beautiful young man in her bed is pathetic, conjured up out of her loneliness and psychosis. Hence, at the end, the widow Holly resembles Anna from Williams's earlier "Oriflamme," whose manic stroll through an expressionistic St. Louis dramatizes her inability to live in the world as it is.

If Williams meant for us to read the story in this way, and I think he did, then we must also acknowledge his daring: to arrive at one theme (the pessimistic one) through its deliberately flawed opposite (the theme of Christ's salvation). In this story, as elsewhere in his period of decline, it was not always Williams's inventiveness that failed him. Indeed, there is much to admire in "The Coming of Something to the Widow Holly," especially a keener and more varied sense of humor than Williams had heretofore demonstrated: slapstick (the furniture and dishware that seem perpetually to fly about the rooming house during the boarders' battles), grotesque black humor (the dead rat that Miss Domingo drops in the bag of her irritating cousin as a departing gift), and verbal wit (Miss Domingo's *"medium*-sized box" of explosives [my italics; 331]).

Although Williams's inventiveness does not fail him in the story, his ability to focus that inventiveness does. Rather than creating a coherent whole, Williams seems not to have known precisely what sort of story he wanted to write. In the first quarter of the story—by far the best—Williams seems intent on painting a profound and complex portrait of a woman cut off by age from her past, with only death to look forward to. But then the focus shifts to the boarders, who are closer to cartoon figures than to believable characters. A. Rose enters momentarily, then drops from sight as the focus returns to the boarders. Their largely comic escapades take up a good half of the story. After the explosion (which, as in a cartoon, destroys the house but harms no one inside), they simply pack up and leave. We hardly miss them because they have been totally irrelevant all along. At this point A. Rose returns as Christopher D. Cosmos, a banal figure no matter how we interpret the ending.

The most obvious result of this meandering focus is an inconsistent tone. Williams's comic touch is entertaining, but what, one might ask, is particularly comic about the widow's plight? Voltaire said that life is a comedy for those who think and a tragedy for those who feel. Williams had written about his fugitives with great feeling during his mature years; his greatness lies in the poetry of his language and the reader's sense of the abundant and genuine feeling suffusing his fiction and drama. Perhaps such great feeling became too much of an emotional burden for Williams, for over the years of his decline, that sense of empathy often gives way to a bitter or farcical wit, either inappropriate to his themes or based on too shallow an intellectual foundation, or both. As in "The Coming of Something to the Widow Holly," in the later stories the comic touch can be, in itself, entertaining, and on rare occasions Williams incorporates comedy into a passably good story. More characteristically, however, the wit and the stories are shallow and more irritating than engaging. Good (or *bad*) examples are "Miss Coynte of Greene," "The Killer Chicken and the Closet Queen," which is every bit as bad as the title would lead one to believe, and "The Knightly Quest," the longest piece in Williams's *Collected Stories*, and one of the worst.

Two other problems in "The Coming of Something to the Widow Holly" prefigure regrettable tendencies in Williams's later stories. One is a tendency toward allegory. Kafka and Borges showed us that allegory can be employed in profound and complex ways. In the hands of lesser writers, however, allegory tends to be shallow and predictable. On this count at least Williams must be considered a lesser writer. His allegory tends to be not only shallow but evasive, as if he were no longer willing or able to wrestle with the complex problems of the human condition. Suffering from tired allegorical impulses are "The Knightly Quest," "The Mattress by the Tomato Patch," and "A Recluse and His Guest," among others.

Related to both the slapstick and the allegorical impulses in "The Coming of Something to the Widow Holly" and later stories is shallow characterization. Allegorical figures, like Christopher D. Cosmos, tend to be *merely* symbolic and incapable of engaging us emotionally or intellectually for very long. Similarly, the cartoonish boarders are entertaining, but not for very long. A greater and more disturbing problem is the widow Holly. From the excellent opening paragraph of the story, one has reason to hope that Williams's portrait of the widow will be a rich one, but she is developed very little after that. Introducing a potentially interesting character but then failing to develop that character and situation to a satisfactory depth is a problem that plagues almost every story over the period of Williams's decline. For some stories, the problem causes them to be merely good when they could have been much better. Other stories—"Das Wasser Ist Kalt" and "Mother Yaws" among them—are simply awful.

"Hard Candy."   Although it is important to understand the exact terms of a once-great writer's decline, the foregoing catalog of sins should not blind us to the fact that Williams did manage to write some interesting stories during his later years, and even an occasional failure possesses some feature worth noting.

One of the more interesting stories of the later years is "Hard Candy," essentially a revision of the earlier "The Mysteries of the Joy Rio." Since "The Mysteries of the Joy Rio" ranks with Williams's best, it would be difficult for "Hard Candy" to be much of an improvement on it. Indeed, the later version is weaker than the former in almost every respect, although it is still quite interesting in its own right.

More important than the relative merits of the stories, perhaps, are the changes that Williams chose to make and what those changes indicate about his predilections as a writer in his years of decline. In general, "Hard Candy" is a harsher story than its predecessor. Pablo, the gentle, sympathetic protagonist of "The Mysteries of the Joy Rio," gives way to old Mr. Krupper, who is not quite cruel to his poor relations but not quite *not* cruel and with whom we do not much sympathize or even much *like*. Pablo's and Krupper's fates are similar in purely factual terms: both die in the balcony of the Joy Rio. Pablo's death, however, is presented elegiacally and lovingly, while Krupper's death is evoked ironically and obscenely: he chokes to death during or after oral sex (the metaphoric hard candy of the title) with a young transient.

It is not the homosexual act itself that is "hard" and obscene in the story—Pablo performs precisely the same acts, after all—but the cold, ironic presentation of the act. Occasionally in "The Mysteries of the Joy Rio," the narrator stood back from the action and commented on the writing of the story, not a particularly wise decision on Williams's part even then, I think, but not intrusive enough to be harmful. In "Hard Candy," though, the narrator constantly distances himself from the action, not mythically or elegiacally, as in most of Williams's earlier stories, but ironically and intrusively. At the worst, the intrusiveness results in awkward prose: "That is what we are going to do, but first we are going to orient ourselves a little more specifically in time, for although these visits of Mr. Krupper to the Joy Rio are events of almost timeless repetition, our story is the narrative of one particular time and involving another individual, both of which must first be established, together, before we resume the company of Mr. Krupper" (341). Even at the best, however, this regrettable narrative approach imparts a coldness to characters and events that prevents the reader from becoming more involved in the action. Certain writers can employ this detached, cold approach quite effectively; Williams never could. "You know, I can never be a true misanthrope," Williams said in his *Memoirs*.[25] Too often in his years of decline he seems to be trying to be just that. The result is almost always disappointing.

Several Near Misses

The stories most worthy of attention in Williams's later years are, logically, those in which he most nearly avoids the unfortunate tendencies that plague him elsewhere during this period.

The two stories that follow "Hard Candy" had the potential to be quite interesting. "Man Bring This Up Road" is a story of starved passion, failed art, and approaching age and death. Williams thought enough of its possibilities to turn it into a full-length play *(The Milk Train Doesn't Stop Here Anymore)*. In turning his attention to the play, however, Williams left the story with its potential unfulfilled. It reads too much like just what it is: a sketch for later, fuller treatment. (The play, unfortunately, was a failure, too.) Like "Man Bring This Up Road," Williams's next story, "The Mattress by the Tomato Patch," has potential that seems largely unrealized. In the former, Williams introduces a complex theme that begs for more complex characters and further development; in the latter, he creates an interesting character—the virtual earth goddess Olga—and an evocative setting—Santa Monica in the early 1940s—but the story remains largely static, little more than a promising character sketch upon which is superimposed a thin allegorical impulse.

The next story, "The Kingdom of Earth," is more successful. The story concerns Chicken, a young man who tends a farm alone until his older brother, Lot, returns with his new bride, the ex-prostitute Myrtle. Lot is dying of tuberculosis, and Chicken, who is illegitimate, fears that the farm will be left to Myrtle. One can guess what direction the action will take. Chicken and Myrtle become enamored of one another, and Lot dies "bawling" their names as they make love. Chicken and Myrtle live, apparently, happily ever after. The story recalls "Twenty-seven Wagons Full of Cotton" in the setting, the mythic impulse, and the rapaciousness of the characters. It does not, however, have the classic leanness of plot that marked "Twenty-seven Wagons Full of Cotton," nor the richness of the major stories from the mature years.

It is not, therefore, in the class of the dozen or so of Williams's best stories.

However, the story is entertainingly comic at times, and it is thought-provoking. Myrtle and Chicken do not get their just desserts, in a traditional moral sense; what they get at the end is something as close to happiness as is ever achieved by Williams's characters. What is the relationship between morality (whose conventions are grossly violated by Chicken and Myrtle), religion (and the story is filled with religious allusions), and happiness? The story's last lines give us Chicken's answer. "And after all, what does anyone know about the Kingdom of Heaven? It's earth I'm after and now I am honest about it and don't pretend I'm nothing but what I am, a lustful creature determined on satisfaction and likely as not to get my full share of it" (378).

Like "The Kingdom of Earth," "Happy August the Tenth" recalls a much earlier story, in this case "The Vine." Both "The Vine" and "Happy August the Tenth" are constructed in two movements: the longer early movement in which the characters are so unsympathetic that the reader hardly cares about their fate, followed by a briefer concluding scene where we suddenly see the pathetic characters with the compassion that they finally elicit. It is a dangerous strategy and not entirely successful in either story, but at least "Happy August the Tenth" is an improvement on the bitter, shallow satires that dominate too much of Williams's later years.

Much the same can be said for "Sabbatha and Solitude," one of the most autobiographical stories of Williams's later years, filled with the anguish of an aging writer facing the loss of his skills, lover, and, ultimately, his life.

In this case the writer, Sabbatha, is a woman, but that fact does not prevent us from seeing her as Williams himself, who frequently identified with his female characters.[26] The painful circumstances that she faces surely were faced, or at least feared, we are convinced, by Williams. Her latest collection of sonnets is trashed by an editor; she is abandoned by her gigolo lover; her table, heretofore reserved for her at the best restaurant, is usurped by a younger, ascendant poet; her obituary, shown to her by a journalist friend, is brief and inaccurate. On top of all this, the poet suffers from arthritis, and when her lover returns—after being gang-raped by ten men—he finds her crawling along the ground like a snake.

Here, where it seems that things could not get much bleaker, the story ends in a strange, irrational, almost flippant sort of affirmation.

How do we arrive at such a paradoxical destination, given the course of the story? Such questions cannot always be answered in life or in art, especially in the art of a romantic like Williams. At the beginning of the last section of the story, the narrator asks the oldest question of all and gives an answer that makes no more sense than the upbeat ending, but one that rings true. "How to go on? You go on, in solitude" (516). This existential affirmation, bleak as it is courageous, is offered before the lover returns. Sabbatha has suffered life's worst but still chooses life. The lover's return, then, seems almost in the nature of a reward for heroism; therefore, the strangely upbeat ending makes some sense.

The dialogue in "Sabbatha and Solitude" is sophomorically scatological at times, and in general the story lacks the poetry and richness of superior efforts from Williams's mature years. Still, the complexity of the theme at least invites us to contemplate Sabbatha and her fate—an inclination that too often eludes Williams's readers during his decline.

"Completed."   The last of Williams's stories that deserves much attention[27] is "Completed," which is the final installment in what we might call the "Rose trilogy" of stories—"Portrait of a Girl in Glass" and "The Resemblance between a Violin Case and a Coffin" being the first two.

Here, Rose becomes Rosemary: Rose plus the Virgin Mary, with the emphasis on virgin. Rosemary has, in fact, reached the end of her teenage years without experiencing menstruation. Despite this biological fact and her pathological shyness, Rosemary's mother, Miss Sally McCool, insists on formally presenting her to the local (Vicksburg, Mississippi) society, which "amounts to publicly announcing that she is now eligible for union in marriage and the bearing of offspring" (519).

The situation is, of course, only a variation on the public recital in "The Resemblance between a Violin Case and a Coffin," and the results are predictably disastrous. The public humiliation[28] does not conclude the story, however; it occurs approximately halfway through. After the debacle, Rosemary spends some time with her Aunt Ella. She returns to her home only briefly, menstruates for the first time, then flees back to Aunt Ella's where she will remain, it is implied, forever.

Aunt Ella is a kindly soul and a kindred spirit of sorts, herself a virgin but a defiant one, resigned to life as a virtual hermit. One senses that

Rosemary has finally found where she belongs, so the story might be said to be an affirmation of sorts. But is it? In fact, "Completed" is the most abjectly pessimistic of the Rose stories. Aunt Ella may be kind, but her kindness is a pitifully meager substitute for love and passion. She may seem defiant in her withdrawal from the world, but that withdrawal is based upon an assumption—"the more that the world outside is excluded, the more the interior world has space in which to increase" (524)—which sounds good but is in fact totally spurious. There is no evidence, none, that Aunt Ella's interior world has increased or that Rosemary's is at all likely to. In fact, the more closely we examine Aunt Ella, the more pitiful she becomes—witness for example the fact that she must take morphine every night and thus spends half of her life so drugged that she can barely see or hear. By the end of the story, even Rosemary understands that Aunt Ella's house is more a trap than a sanctuary: "And it was not until Susie's [the maid's] departing footsteps faded from hearing that Rosemary knew what had happened to her. Aunt Ella had taken her captive. For a moment she thought of resisting" (526).

She does not resist, of course. She will stay with Aunt Ella forever. Giving up the world, imprisoned in a comfortable dwelling, cared for by kindly attendants, drugged against truths that come in the night (Rosemary takes a morphine tablet at the very end)—it is not so very different from life with a lobotomy, after all.

"Completed" is far from as fine a story as "Portrait of a Girl in Glass" or "The Resemblance between a Violin Case and a Coffin." The writing has none of the poetry of the earlier stories. The characterization is generally unconvincing. Miss Sally is a caricature of Mother in "Portrait of a Girl in Glass," and Aunt Ella is no more than a cipher. Nor has Williams totally avoided the tendency toward superficial satire that plagued him throughout his decline. (Rosemary, who has not begun to menstruate, is paired at her coming-out party with Pip, whose testes have not descended.)

Even granting its flaws, however, "Completed" is interesting for giving us one last, and significantly altered, perspective on the Rose archetype. Gone from the story is Rose's beauty; gone is the elegiac tone, the nostalgia, the wistfulness. Also gone from the story, most significantly, is Tom, who narrated the first two stories in the trilogy from a close enough proximity, emotionally if not physically, to sympathize and identify with Rose. Here, the story is told with a rather cynical omniscience, and we can no longer even pity Rose, as the narrator acknowledges. "There was something about Rosemary that drew no sympathy toward her, neither among her elders, nor those of her own generation or younger" (520).

Rather than evoking compassion from the reader, Rosemary makes us uncomfortable, as if we were watching some frail animal, hit by a car, writhing obscenely in its death throes. We wish, more than anything, for the animal to die. We wish, Rosemary wishes, even Williams, we feel, wishes that Rose would just die. The only thing that Rosemary does admirably in the entire story is her high school essay titled "My Purpose in Life." Her succinct response, for which she received an A+: "I HAVE NO PURPOSE IN LIFE EXCEP COMPLETE IT QUIK AS POSIBLE FOR ALL CONSERNED IF ANY BESIDE MY ANT ELLA" (521). It was not completed quickly, unfortunately; she went on to live with her Aunt Ella. But that was just another kind of death.

One senses in reading "Completed" that Williams had grown tired of his subject. In fact, although it is hardly a scholarly analysis of a writer's decline, tired may be as good a diagnosis as any of why Williams's talents seemed to fail him increasingly over the last three decades of his life. Few writers in American literature have explored a single theme—the fate of the "fugitive kind" in a harsh world—as magnificently and to such varied effects as Tennessee Williams. Toward the end he could no longer bring fresh approaches to that theme, and maybe he was just weary of it.

Moreover, it is possible that many readers who are not themselves writers fail to understand what demands writing makes on an author's intellectual, emotional, and even physical capabilities. Williams abused himself so much with alcohol, drugs, and a generally destructive life-style that one marvels that he even *lived* past the 1960s. He was a tired writer when he wrote "Completed" in 1973, and although he lived another ten years, for all practical purposes he was by then completed himself.

Williams's Short Fiction
in Retrospect

In an ideal world an author's stature would be shaped by his merits alone. In actuality, a writer's historical standing is determined to a great extent by literary critics. To be fair to critics—I am one, after all—I think they do, taken as a whole, get it right eventually, most of the time. They seem to have more trouble with some writers than others, though, and unfortunately Tennessee Williams is one of those writers with whom they have trouble. Even so, if we are attempting to assess what Williams's place in the history of the American short story is and likely will be, it will not do to ignore the critics, however much one may occasionally disagree with them.

Part of the problem critics have with Williams the short story writer may stem indirectly from their trouble assessing him as a playwright. Some consider him America's greatest playwright; most claim for him a place at least among the top two or three. Even those who praise him highly, however, seem a little uncomfortable assigning Williams such a lofty position, largely because the last two decades of his career—after *The Night of the Iguana* (1961)—saw him fail again and again in his efforts for the stage. Two decades of failure—indeed, the greater portion of his career—is awfully hard to overlook. This growing dissatisfaction with Williams's plays may have influenced, logically or not, critical reception of his short stories.

A much greater problem, though, as I have noted in the Preface, is that critics too often have ignored his short stories altogether, or at least in large part, in favor of his plays. Even in book-length studies of Williams's work, scholars tend to begrudgingly acknowledge the short fiction. The record for scant attention probably belongs to Felicia Londré, who in *Tennessee Williams*, by my count, devotes one-and-a-half sentences to the short stories, out of nearly two hundred pages of commentary. Not much more promising is the comment by Benjamin Nelson, who notes in the preface to his *Tennessee Williams: The Man and His Work* that Williams is "important as a playwright and poet in his own right"[29]; in other words, Nelson apparently considers Williams's efforts in the short story not worth mentioning. When Nelson finally does get around to addressing the short stories, his stated goal—to "comment upon Williams' treatment in these tales of the themes which are prevalent in the body of his plays"[30]—quite clearly shows the subordinate status, for Nelson, of the stories to the plays. The most fatuous and condescending assessment of the short fiction belongs to Brooks Atkinson. "What does a dramatist do when he has finished his play . . .? He writes short stories, articles, or a journal, or perhaps letters to his friends. He must write something."[31]

It is not my purpose to argue that the short stories deserve more attention than the plays or even attention equal to the plays. I would argue, however, that Tennessee Williams's best short stories are better than all but a few of his plays, certainly more deserving of attention than most of the plays written in the last two decades of his life. At the very least, it can hardly be disputed that critical neglect makes difficult the task of assessing Williams's place in the development of the American short story.

I do not mean to imply by these comments that the short stories of Tennessee Williams are waiting to be discovered. By as early as 1955, in a review of *One Arm and Other Stories*, William Peden noted: "At his best, as he is in at least two or three of these stories, Tennessee Williams is in a class by himself. Even at his worst he creates magical, terrifying, and unforgettable effects; his only limitations appear to be self-imposed."[32] Two decades later, in a 1974 review of *Eight Mortal Ladies Possessed: A Book of Stories*, Peden continued to champion Williams's cause. "Such stories as 'The Field of Blue Children,' 'Three Players of a Summer Game,' 'Portrait of a Girl in Glass,' 'The Resemblance between a Violin Case and a Coffin,' and half a dozen others are of their kind as good as anything produced during recent years."[33]

William Peden is not alone in his high regard for Williams's short stories. In contrast to the tendency noted earlier for critics to ignore Williams's short stories in favor of the plays, a smaller but significant number of critics share a view that can best be summarized in a comment by Robert Phillips, from a review of Williams's *Collected Stories*. "Had he written nothing else, Williams' stories would be sufficient evidence of his bid for fame."[34]

Another observation from that same review by Phillips is equally interesting: the *Collected Stories* "belongs on the shelf with Eudora Welty's and Flannery O'Connor's collected stories."[35] Such a comment acknowledges a second duty of critics: not just to determine relative merit but also to determine *place*. Where, in the tradition of the short story, does Williams's work belong?

Critics generally address this problem in one of two ways: either they assign Williams to a pigeonhole too narrow to contain him comfortably, or they throw up their hands and exclaim, "What *is* one to make of him?" The latter response, I think, is not totally inappropriate because none of the pigeonholes works very well. Most recently, Williams's status as a homosexual writer has been emphasized. Although the homosexual themes are important and interesting in his short stories, especially since he generally avoided them in his plays, surely this label is absurdly narrow for a writer of Williams's expansive and profound sympathies.

A more frequently applied label—implied in Robert Phillips's placing Williams's stories next to Welty's and O'Connor's—is "Southern writer." Certainly, Williams thought of himself as Southern, and a number of his stories are set in the South. However, in only a few of the stories—"Big Black: A Mississippi Idyll" and "Twenty-seven Wagons Full of Cotton," for instance—is the Southern setting crucial. In fact, in many of the others set in Southern locales—especially New Orleans stories such as "In Memory of an Aristocrat" and "The Angel in the Alcove"—the Southern setting is of minor importance. They probably could have been set in Mexico or Italy with little harm. (Indeed, the free life-style for which Williams admired New Orleans is hardly a Southern characteristic.)

Far more important than Mississippi or New Orleans in Williams's stories, and in his life, is St. Louis. Historically and sociologically, St. Louis has certain Southern ties, but it could easily be classified as a midwestern industrial city, more akin to Cleveland or Milwaukee than to New Orleans or, certainly, Columbus, Mississippi. Whatever *we* think of St. Louis, Tennessee Williams did not consider St. Louis Southern. It was "St. Pollution" and that "northern city."

Southern, it must be admitted, implies more than a geographical context. Especially in Southern fiction we have come to expect violence and the grotesque, and these may be found in Williams's stories. Violence is no more prevalent in Williams's stories than in Hemingway's or Hawthorne's, however, and Williams's grotesques are as closely akin to Sherwood Anderson's emotional grotesques as they are to Flannery O'Connor's twisted figures. While I do not object to the

"Southern" label for Williams, I find it only partially useful and cannot help surmising that Williams would far less frequently be mentioned as a southern writer had he stuck with the name Tom rather than adopting the misleading "Tennessee."

"Homosexual" and "Southern" are the two labels most frequently applied to Williams and his stories, but other labels are occasionally used. One of the most interesting observations was made by Reynolds Price in a review of the *Collected Stories*. "By the mid-1940's to early 50's, he was attempting stories that, while still grounded in personal experience, abound in the kind of magic realism so widely believed to have originated in Latin America."[36] As Price implies, scholars often give Latin American writers such as Gabriel García Marquez and Julio Cortázar too much credit for *inventing* magic realism (essentially, the interpolation of the supernatural into a realistic context), when the strategy is at least as old as Homer. Williams, antedating both García Marquez and Cortázar, does use a variety of magic realism in such stories as "The Mysteries of the Joy Rio," "The Angel in the Alcove," and "The Malediction," and Price is to be commended for reminding us of this fact. Williams does not use the strategy often enough or characteristically enough to be classified as a magic-realist author, however—nor is Price claiming such a place for him.

Thus, for one reason or another, the major categories into which Williams's work is placed are only partially helpful. What, then, are we to do with him?

To claim that Williams is sui generis is tempting but evasive. No author develops or works in a vacuum. Each author is influenced by his predecessors and shares affinities with cetain contemporaries.

Williams himself acknowledged the influence of Chekhov and D. H. Lawrence (along with Strindberg and Ibsen in reference more specifically to drama). We noted earlier in this study that "The Mysteries of the Joy Rio" and "The Angel in the Alcove" recall Chekhov's fiction, and other stories could easily be added to the list. Moreover, Lawrence's interest in sexual and spiritual liberation would obviously be attractive to Williams, and most of his stories reflect some aspect of this theme.

It is possible, however, that the work of other short story writers is even closer to Williams's than is Chekhov's and Lawrence's, although whether or not they can be considered influences is debatable. One,

William Faulkner, seems an obvious choice considering the two authors' Southern roots. But the specifically Southern aspect seems to me less important than something harder to define: a certain expansiveness of vision and breadth of sympathies rarely found in short story writers, even the better ones. While one would hesitate to call Faulkner's protagonists fugitives in quite the sense that Williams used, both writers were fond of focusing on characters in their terrible isolation—think of Faulkner's "A Rose for Emily," "That Evening Sun," and "Dry September"—yet making that isolation operate within a social and cultural context. This expansiveness is not precisely the same in the two authors—Faulkner's tends to be richly historical and Williams's evocatively mythic—yet it is there nevertheless.

One might surmise that this expansiveness is shared by all great writers, but such is not the case. Franz Kafka might be said to represent the opposite extreme: that is, his protagonists operate outside any identifiable context except their own claustrophobic alienation.

To point out similarities between the work of Faulkner and Williams may seem natural and appropriate; to do so in reference to Nikolai Gogol may seem bizarre. Yet as different as they at first appear, one gropes to find an author whose short stories more resemble Williams's in certain fundamental ways than do Gogol's. The expansiveness of vision and breadth of sympathies noted earlier also belong to Gogol, who characteristically dramatized the plight of individuals of a certain class operating in a social and historical context: "The Nose" and "The Overcoat," for instance. Moreover, the magic realism in Williams's work, noted by Reynolds Price, is obviously present in Gogol's. Even more important, because it is less often found in Southern writers, is both writers' penchant for satire and allegory. The difference in the quality of their satire is unfortunate; Gogol is a master satirist, whereas blatant satire almost always fails in Williams. However, like it or not, satire is a major component in Williams's work, increasingly so over the years.

Perhaps even closer to Williams's short fiction than Gogol's is that of Williams's good friend Carson McCullers. McCullers shares with Williams the Southern heritage, lyrical prose style, mythic scope, occasional use of violent and grotesque materials, and the two-edged dagger: the theme of loneliness and destructive passions. All these come together in McCullers's masterpiece, "The Ballad of the Sad Cafe." This marvelous tale is the product of McCullers's special and distinctive genius, yet one senses that it is near enough to Williams's creative heart that he himself could almost have written it. And while one struggles to envision Faulkner or Gogol having a try at "One Arm" or "The Mysteries of the Joy Rio," Carson McCullers—perhaps so.

Noting similarities between Williams's work and that of three widely disparate authors—at least Gogol rests rather uncomfortably with Faulkner and McCullers—is not the same thing as placing Williams in a historical and literary context, of course. Determining the proper context for Williams is difficult, partly because his short fiction belongs to a period of transition for American literature in general and the short story in particular.

By the 1940s and early 1950s, the period in which Williams wrote most of his best short stories, the majority of the short fiction of the great American modernists—Faulkner, Hemingway, Sherwood Anderson, Katherine Anne Porter—was behind them. At the same time, no group of short story writers seemed ready to take up the torch. Though in retrospect we note that there were some fine short stories written in that period, still, literary history is almost certain to see the forties and early fifties as a period of relative stagnation. The much ballyhooed renaissance in the American short story did not begin until much later, in the seventies, and by then Williams, unfortunately, was not writing good enough fiction to be considered a part of it.

So what are we left with, then? Williams the transitional Southern homosexual? Very likely, that is exactly what Williams's position will be, rightly or wrongly, in the tradition of the American short story. Moreover, one must admit that although the pigeonholes are far too restrictive, they do contain some truth.

The whole concept of context is interesting and ephemeral. One might do well to consider the difficulty critics and readers had placing Proust, Joyce, Kafka, Faulkner, and Borges when those great writers first made their presences felt. Critics simply did not know what to make of them, and it was the writers themselves who created their own contexts by their massive influence on their contemporaries and succeeding generations. (And in "Kafka and His Precursors," Borges, in one of his delightful, maddening paradoxes, insists that a great writer creates his own *predecessors*.) Williams is no more singular a short story writer than Kafka or Borges—no more singular, indeed, than Hemingway or Faulkner, if we remember how innovative those writers seemed at their first appearance—but he has been less influential as a short story writer and thus has not created his own context of fellow writers.

Had he written his stories two decades sooner, Tennessee Williams might have gone down in history as one of our greatest short story writers. His technical range is greater, by far, than Hemingway's or Sherwood Anderson's. His sense of character and narrative is at least as profound as Katherine Anne Porter's. His passion for humanity and his ability to dramatize that passion are unsurpassed by any writer.

Great as his range was, however, virtually everything he did had been done before, and better, by William Faulkner. In addition, profound as his sympathies and sense of character were, as admirable as his narrative talents were, he can lay no exclusive claim to these. Moreover, if we wanted to read stories in which the South is dramatized, surely we would go to Faulkner first, and among Faulkner's successors probably O'Connor and Welty, perhaps even McCullers, before Williams.

Where does this leave Williams? Where he always felt himself to be: a fugitive even among his contemporaries, not quite fitting in but creating memorable fiction out of the profound realization of that very fact. How large Williams's place will be in the history of the American short story is debatable, but that a place exists, and securely so, seems to me certain. Williams likely would find ironic the possibility that he would be embraced by the world only after his death. But he would understand.

Notes to Part 1

1. Gore Vidal, introduction to *Tennessee Williams: Collected Stories* (New York: New Directions, 1985), xx.

2. Williams wrote dozens of stories, especially during his teenage years but also later, that do not appear in his *Collected Stories*. I have proceeded under the assumption that these unpublished stories are not essential to an understanding of Williams's development as a short story writer and have not included them for discussion in this study. (The *Collected Stories* does include a number of previously unpublished stories; I do discuss a few of these.)

All references to Williams's stories, unless otherwise specified, are to *Tennessee Williams: Collected Stories* and will hereafter be cited in the text.

3. Notes to *Tennessee Williams: Collected Stories*, 574.

4. Quoted in Gore Vidal's introduction to *Tennessee Williams: Collected Stories*, xxiii.

5. "The Life and Ideas of Tennessee Williams," *P.M.*, 6 May 1945, 7.

6. Notes to *Collected Stories*, 571.

7. See Gary Spoto, *The Kindness of Strangers: The Life of Tennessee Williams* (Boston: Little, Brown, 1985), 48ff., for a discussion of various pressures affecting Williams at this time.

8. Spoto, *Kindness of Strangers*, 337.

9. Eugene B. Griesman, "Williams: A Rebellious Puritan," *Chicago Sun-Times*, 27 Mar. 1983, 4.

10. Quoted in Spoto, *Kindness of Strangers*, 52.

11. See Spoto, *Kindness of Strangers*, 35ff., for a discussion of this period in Williams's life.

12. Throughout this study, unless otherwise specified, I am using for the year of composition the dates provided in *Tennessee Williams: Collected Stories*. According to Donald Spoto (see *Kindness of Strangers*, 80), Williams may have written a draft of "The Mysteries of the Joy Rio" as early as 1939. Williams endlessly revised stories, even after their publication sometimes, so it is often difficult to be very precise about when a story was written.

13. Spoto, *Kindness of Strangers*, 167.

14. Spoto, *Kindness of Strangers*, 400.

15. The climactic scene in the movie version of the play contains just such a calamity.

16. In his essay "The Man in the Overstuffed Chair," which prefaces *Tennessee Williams: Collected Stories*, Williams recalls that it was his father who "taught [him] to hate," for which he has managed to forgive him. "Sometimes I wonder," he says, however, "if I have forgiven my mother for teaching me to expect more love from the world, more softness in it, than I could ever offer" (xv). Also interesting is Williams's recollection that a psychiatrist once told him that "you will begin to forgive the world when you've forgiven your father" (xv). Perhaps "Portrait of a Girl in Glass" implies at least the potential for that forgiveness.

17. Walter Wagner, "Playwright as Individual: A Conversation with Tennessee Williams," *Playbill* 3 (Mar. 1966).

18. Once again, the chronology is ambiguous. Williams began writing "Desire and the Black Masseur" in 1942, so it could be seen as an earlier work than "The Interval" or "Tent Worms." He did not complete it until 1946, however, so it might be seen as a later story than the two aforementioned. It follows the two in *Complete Stories*, and once again I defer to that collection's chronology.

19. Spoto, *Kindness of Strangers*, 123.

20. See Spoto, *Kindness of Strangers*, for the autobiographical backgrounds to the story (19–22) and for Cornelius Williams's reaction at its publication (163–64).

21. See Vidal, introduction to *Collected Stories*, xxii.

22. Spoto, *Kindness of Strangers*, 88.

23. See Spoto, *Kindness of Strangers*, 176, for a discussion of Williams's own alcohol problems during the time that the story was written.

24. Once again I am following the arrangement of *Tennessee Williams: Collected Stories*, although one could argue that "The Coming of Something to the Widow Holly" should be considered a much earlier story. Although not finished until 1953, Williams began work on the story as early as 1943.

25. Tennessee Williams, *Memoirs* (Garden City, N.Y.: Doubleday, 1975), 5.

26. The director Luchino Visconti, for instance, habitually called Tennessee "Blanche"—after Blanche DuBois, of course. See Williams's *Memoirs*, caption to illustration number 78.

27. Williams's finest piece of writing during his decline is "Grand," written in the early 1960's and collected in *The Knightly Quest: A Novel and Four Short Stories* (1966). Williams rarely wrote more movingly in any period of his life, and few if any of his characters are more lovingly and vividly rendered than "Grand," the family nickname for Tennessee's maternal grandmother, Rosina Dakin.

As fine as "Grand" is, I hesitate to include it among Williams's best short stories for a purely technical reason: it is not, so far as I can determine, a short story at all. Comparing events in the story to accounts in Williams's *Memoirs* and in Donald Spoto's biography of the author, I fail to find evidence of fictionalizing, of invention. Grand is an actual person, secondary figures are actual people, the events related actually happened and in the way, so far as I can determine, that Williams relates them. Moreover, "Grand" is not constructed around a conflict, the soul of the short story—except for the universal conflict of living and then dying. The account is vividly and emotionally written, but the best essays, history, biography, and autobiography are vividly written, too.

Splitting hairs over what to call "Grand" is perhaps a profitless exercise, although I would note that literary criticism is a discipline that thrives on just such hair-splitting classifications. We can hardly discuss writing without them. Let us leave "Grand," then, where we began this discussion: by noting, with unqualified admiration, that it is a fine piece of writing.

28. For Williams's account of his sister's actual "coming out," in Knoxville, Tennessee, see his *Memoirs*, 116–17.

29. Benjamin Nelson, *Tennessee Williams: The Man and His Work* (New York: Ivan Obolensky, 1961), viii.

30. Nelson, *The Man and His Work*, 186.

31. Brooks Atkinson, review of *The Knightly Quest* by Tennessee Williams, *Saturday Review* 50 (25 Feb. 1967), 53.

32. William Peden, "Broken Apollo and Blasted Dreams," *Saturday Review* 38 (8 Jan. 1955), 11.

33. William Peden, "The Recent American Short Story," *Sewanee Review* 82 (Fall 1974), 725.

34. Robert Phillips, "Evidence for Fame," *Commonweal* 113 (14 Mar. 1986), 156.

35. Phillips, "Evidence for Fame," 156.

36. Reynolds Price, "His Battle Cry Was 'Valor'!" *New York Times Book Review*, 1 Dec. 1985, 11.

Part 2

TENNESSEE WILLIAMS ON WRITING

Introduction

Tennessee Williams was not one of the scholar-writers whom we have become increasingly accustomed to encountering in literature. He was never employed by the universities, which encourage scholarship even from their artists, nor was he intellectually or emotionally inclined toward careful analysis of his craft.

Still, Williams did write a number of interesting essays and reviews on specific writers and writing in general. Equally interesting are the numerous interviews with Williams and his more personal writings: letters and memoirs. As one might predict, the bulk of his comments concern writing plays, but he did occasionally turn his attention to the short story, or at least to writing in general.

The following selections are from three sources. First are three essays. "The Human Psyche—Alone" ostensibly concerns the fiction of Williams's friend Paul Bowles. Bowles's preoccupation, as Williams sees it, with the "spiritual isolation of individual beings," however, could as easily describe Williams himself. In the essay "Introduction to Carson McCullers's *Reflections in a Golden Eye*," Williams addresses the issue of the Southern writer, among other things. In "The World I Live In" Williams interviews himself. Not surprisingly, it is one of his liveliest and most interesting interviews. Another major source of Williams's reflections on writing is his letters to friends and associates. Reprinted here are excerpts from two letters to his good friend Donald Windham. The first provides interesting background on Williams's short story "The Mattress by the Tomato Patch"; the second shows Williams honestly but gently criticizing a friend's story. Williams's *Memoirs* provides another fertile source for his reflections on writing and being a writer, and a number of excerpts from his *Memoirs* conclude this section of autobiographical writings.

The Human Psyche—Alone*

Paul Bowles is a man and author of exceptional latitude but he has, like nearly all serious artists, a dominant theme. That theme is the fearful isolation of the individual being. He is as preoccupied with this isolation as the collectivist writers of ten years ago were concerned with group membership and purposes. Our contemporary American society seems no longer inclined to hold itself open to very explicit criticism from within. This is what we hope and suppose to be a transitory condition that began with the Second World War. It will probably wear itself out, for it is directly counter to the true American nature and tradition, but at the present time it seems to be entering its extreme phase, the all but complete suppression of any dissident voices. What choice has the artist, now, but withdrawal into the caverns of his own isolated being? Hence the outgrowth of the "new school of decadence," so bitterly assailed by the same forces that turned our writers inward? Young men are writing first novels with a personal lyricism much like that exhibited in the early poems of the late Edna St. Vincent Millay, a comparison which is disparaging to neither party nor to the quality itself. For what is youth without lyricism, and what would lyricism be without a personal accent?

But Paul Bowles cannot be accurately classed with these other young men, not only because he is five or ten years older than most of them but because, primarily, a personal lyricism is not what distinguishes his work. His work is distinguished by its mature philosophical content, which is another thing altogether. As I noted in a review of his first novel, *The Sheltering Sky*, Bowles is apparently the only American writer whose work reflects the extreme spiritual dislocation (and a philosophical adjustment to it) of our immediate times. He has "an organic continuity" with the present in a way that is commensurate with the great French trio of Camus, Genet, and Sartre. This does little to improve

*©1978 by Tennessee Williams, from *Where I Live*. Reprinted by permission of New Directions Publishing Corp. This review of Paul Bowles's *The Delicate Prey and Other Stories* appeared in the *Saturday Review of Literature*, 23 December 1950.

his stock with the school of criticism which advocates a literature that is happily insensitive to any shock or abrasion, the sort that would sing "Hail, Hail, the Gang's all Here" while being extricated, still vocally alive, from the debris of a Long Island railroad disaster.

But to revert to the opening observation in this review, Paul Bowles is preoccupied with the spiritual isolation of individual beings. This is not a thing as simple as loneliness. Certainly a terrible kind of loneliness is expressed in most of these stories and in the novel that preceded them to publication, but the isolated beings in these stories have deliberately chosen their isolation in most cases, not merely accepted and endured it. There is a singular lack of human give-and-take, of true emotional reciprocity, in the groups of beings assembled upon his intensely but somberly lighted sets. The drama is that of the single being rather than of beings in relation to each other. Paul Bowles has experienced an unmistakable revulsion from the act of social participation. One may surmise in him the social experience of two decades. Then the withdrawal is logical. The artist is not a man who will advance against a bayonet pressed to his abdomen unless another bayonet is pressed to his back, and even then he is not likely to move forward. He will, if possible, stand still. But Mr. Bowles has discovered that the bayonet is pointed at the man moving forward in our times, and that a retreat is still accessible. He has done the sensible thing under these circumstances. He has gone back into the cavern of himself. These seventeen stories are the exploration of a cavern of individual sensibilities, and fortunately the cavern is a deep one containing a great deal that is worth exploring.

Nowhere in any writing that I can think of has the separateness of the one human psyche been depicted more vividly and shockingly. If one feels that life achieves its highest value and significance in those rare moments—they are scarcely longer than that—when two lives are confluent, when the walls of isolation momentarily collapse between two persons, and if one is willing to acknowledge the possibility of such intervals, however rare and brief and difficult they may be, the intensely isolated spirit evoked by Paul Bowles may have an austerity which is frightening at least. But don't make the mistake of assuming that what is frightening is necessarily inhuman. It is curious to note that the spirit evoked by Bowles in so many of these stories does *not* seem inhuman, nor does it strike me as being antipathetic.

Even in the stories where this isolation is most shockingly, even savagely, stated and underlined the reader may sense an inverted kind of longing and tenderness for the thing whose absence the story concerns. This inverted, subtly implicit kind of tenderness comes out most clearly in one of the less impressive stories of the collection. This story is called "The Scorpion." It concerns an old woman in a primitive society of some obscure kind who has been left to live in a barren cave by her two sons. One of these deserters eventually returns to the cave with the purpose of bringing his mother to the community in which he and his brother have taken up residence. But the old woman is reluctant to leave her cave. The cave, too small for more than one person to occupy, is the only thing in reality that she trusts or feels at home in. It is curtained by rainfall and it is full of scorpions and it is not furnished by any kind of warmth or comfort, yet she would prefer to remain there than to accompany her son, who has finally, for some reason not stated in the story, decided to take her back with him to the community where he has moved. The journey must be made on foot and it will take three days. They finally set out together, but for the old woman there is no joy in the anticipation of a less isolated existence: there is only submission to a will that she does not interpret.

Here is a story that sentimentality, even a touch of it, could have destroyed. But sentimentality is a thing that you will find nowhere in the work of Paul Bowles. When he fails, which is rarely, it is for another reason. It is because now and then his special hardness of perception, his defiant rejection of all things emollient have led him into an area in which a man can talk only to himself.

The volume contains among several fine stories at least one that is a true masterpiece of short fiction—"A Distant Episode," published first in *Partisan Review*. In this story Paul Bowles states the same theme which he developed more fully in his later novel. The theme is the collapse of the civilized "Super Ego" into a state of almost mindless primitivisim, totally dissociated from society except as an object of its unreasoning hostility. It is his extremely powerful handling of this theme again and again in his work which makes Paul Bowles probably the American writer who represents most truly the fierily and blindly explosive world that we live in so precariously from day and night to each uncertain tomorrow.

Introduction to
Carson McCullers's
*Reflections in a Golden Eye**

The reasons for failure to justly evaluate this second novel go beyond the common, temporal disadvantage that all second novels must suffer, and I feel that an examination of these reasons may be of considerably greater pertinence to our aim of suggesting a fresh evaluation.

To quote directly from book notices is virtually impossible, here in Rome where I am writing these comments, but I believe that I am safe in assuming that it was their identification of the author with a certain school of American writers, mostly of Southern origin, that made her subject to a particular and powerful line of attack.

Even in the preceding book some readers must undoubtedly have detected a warning predisposition toward certain elements which are popularly known as "morbid." Doubtless there were some critics, as well as readers, who did not understand why Carson McCullers had elected to deal with a matter so unwholesome as the spiritual but passionate attachment that existed between a deaf-mute and a half-wit. But the tenderness of the book disarmed them. The depth and nobility of its compassion were so palpable that at least for the time being the charge of decadence had to be held in check. This forbearance was of short duration. In her second novel the veil of subjective tenderness, which is the one quality of her talent which she has occasionally used to some excess, was drawn away. And the young writer suddenly flashed in their faces the cabalistic emblems of fellowship with a certain company of writers that the righteous "Humanists" in the world

*©1978 by Tennessee Williams, from *Where I Live*. Reprinted by permission of New Directions Publishing Corp. This essay appeared as the introduction to Carson McCullers's *Reflections in a Golden Eye*, New Directions, 1950.

of letters regarded as the most abhorrent and most necessary to expose and attack.

Not being a follower of literary journals, I am not at all sure what title has been conferred upon this group of writers by their disparaging critics, but for my own convenience I will refer to them as the Gothic school. It has a very ancient lineage, this school, but our local inheritance of its tradition was first brought into prominence by the early novels of William Faulkner, who still remains a most notorious and unregenerate member. There is something in the region, something in the blood and culture, of the Southern state that has somehow made them the center of this Gothic school of writers. Certainly something more important than the influence of a single artist, Faulkner, is to be credited with its development, just as in France the Existentialist movement is surely attributable to forces more significant than the personal influence of Jean-Paul Sartre. There is actually a common link between the two schools, French and American, but characteristically the motor impulse of the French school is intellectual and philosophic while that of the American is more of an emotional and romantic nature. What is this common link? In my opinion it is most simply definable as a sense, an intuition, of an underlying dreadfulness in modern experience.

The question one hears most frequently about writers of the Gothic school is this little classic:

"Why do they write about such *dreadful* things?"

This is a question that escapes not only from the astonished lips of summer matrons who have stumbled into the odd world of William Faulkner, through some inadvertence or mischief at the lending library, but almost as frequently and certainly more importantly, from the pens of some of the most eminent book critics. If it were a solely and typically philistine manifestation, there would be no sense or hope in trying to answer it, but the fact that it is used as a major line of attack by elements that the artist has to deal with—critics, publishers, distributors, not to mention the reading public—makes it a question that we should try seriously to answer or at least understand.

The great difficulty of understanding, and communication, lies in the fact that we who are asked this question and those who ask it do not really inhabit the same universe.

You do not need to tell me that this remark smacks of artistic snobbism which is about as unattractive as any other form that snobbism can take. (If artists are snobs, it is much in the same humble way that lunatics are: not because they wish to be different, and hope and believe that they are, but because they are forever painfully struck in the face with the inescapable fact of their difference which makes them hurt and lonely enough to want to undertake the vocation of artists.)

It appears to me, sometimes, that there are only two kinds of people who live outside what E. E. Cummings has defined as "this so-called world of ours"—the artists and the insane. Of course there are those who are not practicing artists and those who have not been committed to asylums, but who have enough of one or both magical elements, lunacy and vision, to permit them also to slip sufficiently apart from "this so-called world of ours" to undertake or accept an exterior view of it. But I feel that Mr. Cummings established a highly defensible point when he stated, at least by implication, that "the everyday humdrum world, which includes me and you and millions upon millions of men and women" is pretty largely something done with mirrors, and the mirrors are the millions of eyes that look at each other and things no more penetratingly than the physical senses allow. If they are conscious of there being anything to explore beyond this *soi-disant* universe, they comfortably suppose it to be represented by the mellow tones of the pipe organ on Sundays.

In expositions of this sort it is sometimes very convenient to invent an opposite party to an argument, as Mr. Cummings did in making the remarks I have quoted. Such an invented adversary might say to me at this point:

"I have read some of these books, like this one here, and I think they're sickening and crazy. I don't know why anybody should want to write about such diseased and perverted and fantastic creatures and try to pass them off as representative members of the human race! That's how I feel about it. But I do have this sense you talk about, as much as you do or anybody else, this sense of fearfulness or dreadfulness or whatever you want to call it. I read the newspapers and I think it's all pretty awful. I think the atom bomb is awful and I think that the confusion of the world is awful. I think that cancer is fearful, and I certainly don't look forward to the idea of dying, which I think is dreadful. I could go on forever, or at least indefinitely, giving you a list of things that I think are dreadful. And isn't that having what you call the Sense of Dreadfulness or something?"

My hesitant answer would be—"Yes, and no. Mostly no."

And then I would explain a little further, with my usual awkwardness at exposition:

"All of these things that you list as dreadful are parts of the visible, sensible phenomena of every man's experience or knowledge, but the true sense of dread is not a reaction to anything sensible or visible or even, strictly, materially, *knowable*. But rather it's a kind of spiritual intuition of something almost too incredible and shocking to talk about, which underlies the whole so-called thing. It is the uncommunicable something that we shall have to call *mystery* which is so inspiring of dread among these modern artists that we have been talking about. . . ."

Then I pause, looking into the eyes of my interlocutor, which I hope are beginning to betray some desire to believe me, and I say to him, "Am I making any better sense?"

"Maybe. But I can see it's an effort!"

"My friend, you have me where the hair is short."

"But you know, you still haven't explained why these writers have to write about crazy people doing terrible things!"

"You mean the externals they use?"

"'Externals?'"

"You are objecting to their choice of symbols."

"Symbols, are they?"

"Of course. Art is made out of symbols the way your body is made out of vital tissue."

"Then why have they got to use—?"

"Symbols of the grotesque and the violent? Because a book is short and a man's life is long."

"That I don't understand."

"Think it over."

"You mean it's got to be more concentrated?"

"Exactly. The awfulness has to be compressed."

"But can't a writer ever get the same effect without using such God damn awful subjects?"

"I believe one writer did. The greatest of modern times, James Joyce. He managed to get the whole sense of awfulness without resorting to externals that departed on the surface from the ordinary and the familiar. But he wrote very long books, when he accomplished this incredibly difficult thing, and also he used a device that is known as the interior monologue which only he and one other great modern writer could employ without being excessively tiresome."

"What other?"

"Marcel Proust. But Proust did not ever quite dare to deliver the message of Absolute Dread. He was too much of a physical coward. The atmosphere of his work is rather womb-like. The flight into protection is very apparent."

"I guess we've talked long enough. Don't you have to get back to your subject now?"

"I have just about finished with my subject, thanks to you."

"Aren't you going to make a sort of statement that adds it up?"

"Neatly? Yes. Maybe I'd better try: here it is: *Reflections in a Golden Eye* is one of the purest and most powerful of those works which are conceived in that Sense of The Awful which is the desperate black root of nearly all significant modern art, from the *Guernica* of Picasso to the cartoons of Charles Addams. Is that all right?"

"I have quit arguing with you. So long."

The World I Live In*

Tennessee Williams Interviews Himself

Question: Can we talk frankly?

Answer: There's no other way we can talk.

Q: Perhaps you know that when your first successful play, *The Glass Menagerie,* was revived early this season, a majority of the reviewers felt that it was still the best play you have written, although it is now twelve years old?

A: Yes, I read all my play notices and criticisms, even those that say that I write for money and that my primary appeal is to brutal and ugly instincts.

Q: Where there is so much smoke—!

A: A fire smokes the most when you start pouring water on it.

Q: But surely you'll admit that there's been a disturbing note of harshness and coldness and violence and anger in your more recent works?

A: I think, without planning to do so, I have followed the developing tension and anger and violence of the world and time that I live in through my own steadily increasing tension as a writer and person.

Q: Then you admit that this "developing tension," as you call it, is a reflection of a condition in yourself?

A: Yes.

Q: A morbid condition?

A: Yes.

Q: Perhaps verging on the psychotic?

A: I guess my work has always been a kind of psychotherapy for me.

Q: But how can you expect audiences to be impressed by plays and other writings that are created as a release for the tensions of a possible or incipient madman?

A: It releases their own.

Q: Their own what?

A: Increasing tensions, verging on the psychotic.

Q: You think the world's going mad?

A: Going? I'd say nearly gone! As the Gypsy said in *Camino Real*, the world is a funny paper read backwards. And that way it isn't so funny.

Q: How far do you think you can go with this tortured view of the world?

A: As far as the world can go in its tortured condition, maybe that far, but no further.

Q: You don't expect audiences and critics to go along with you, do you?

A: No.

Q: Then why do you push and pull them that way?

A: I go that way. I don't push or pull anyone with me.

Q: Yes, but you hope to continue to have people listen to you, don't you?

A: Naturally I hope to.

Q: Even if you throw them off by the violence and horror of your works?

A: Haven't you noticed that people are dropping all around you, like moths out of season, as the result of the present plague of violence and horror in this world and time that we live in?

Q: But you're an entertainer, with artistic pretensions, and people are not entertained any more by cats on hot tin roofs and Baby Dolls and passengers on crazy streetcars!

A: Then let them go to the musicals and the comedies. I'm not going to change my ways. It's hard enough for me to write what I want to write without me trying to write what you say they want me to write which I don't want to write.

Q: Do you have any positive message, in your opinion?

A: Indeed I do think that I do.

Q: Such as what?

A: The crying, almost screaming, need of a great world-wide human effort to know ourselves and each other a great deal better, well enough to concede that no man has a monopoly on right or virtue any more than any man has a corner on duplicity and evil and so forth. If people, and races and nations, would start with that self-manifest truth, then I think that the world could sidestep the sort of corruption which I have involuntarily chosen as the basic, allegorical theme of my plays as a whole.

Q: You sound as if you felt quite detached and superior to this process of corruption in society.

A: I have never written about any kind of vice which I can't observe in myself.

Q: But you accuse society, as a whole, of succumbing to a deliberate mendacity, and you appear to find yourself separate from it as a writer.

A: As a writer, yes, but not as a person.

Q: Do you think this is a peculiar virtue of yours as a writer?

A: I'm not sentimental about writers. But I'm inclined to think that most writers, and most other artists, too, are primarily motivated in their desperate vocation by a desire to find and to separate truth from the complex of lies and evasions they live in, and I think that this impulse is what makes their work not so much a profession as a vocation, a true "calling."

Q: Why don't you write about nice people? Haven't you ever known any nice people in your life?

A: My theory about nice people is so simple that I am embarrassed to say it.

Q: Please say it!

A: Well, I've never met one that I couldn't love if I completely knew him and understood him, and in my work I have at least tried to arrive at knowledge and understanding.

I don't believe in "original sin." I don't believe in "guilt." I don't believe in villians or heroes—only right or wrong ways that individuals have taken, not by choice but by necessity or by certain still-uncomprehended influences in themselves, their circumstances, and their antecedents.

This is so simple I'm ashamed to say it, but I'm sure it's true. In fact, I would bet my life on it! And that's why I don't understand why our propaganda machines are always trying to teach us, to persuade us, to hate and fear other people on the same little world that we live in.

Why don't we meet these people and get to know them as I try to meet and know people in my plays? This sounds terribly vain and egotistical.

I don't want to end on such a note. Then what shall I say? That I know that I am a minor artist who has happened to write one or two major works? I can't even say which they are. It doesn't matter. I have said my say. I may still say it again, or I may shut up now. It doesn't depend on you, it depends entirely on me, and the operation of chance or Providence in my life.

Excerpts from Letters to Donald Windham, 1940–65*

[Dear Donnie:]

Zola the Landlady has given me a bowl of ripe tomatoes from the garden back of the house. They are big as your fist, bloody red, and spurt between your teeth when you bite into them. Bits of brown earth are still clinging about the spiky leaves and stems and they taste like the sweetness and pride of all unconscious life which we put so shamelessly to our own uses. Zola is a wonderful character, a lecherous communist woman of about forty-five with a great blown-up body. She sleeps with any man in the house who will have her, and has a frail, sour little husband named Ernie who does all the house-work, bed-making, Etc., while she soaks up the sun on the porch steps or a big raggedy mattress she has flung out in the back-yard near the tomato patch, with a cocker spaniel resting its head on her belly. Right now the wrestling champion of the Pacific coast is stopping here, a big monolith of a body. He stalks down the hall in an electric blue satin robe clinging like a kiss to all the lines of his body and lounges in the hall telephoning his women. While he phones he shifts his body in the glittering robe lasciviously from right to left, the big buttocks jutting out and rolling as he croons into the mouth-piece. He fairly fucks the wall. I always pretend to be waiting to make a call so I can watch, and tonight Zola finally and reluctantly introduced us. Either she has gotten all of it she can take or can't get it. There are two things we agree on, and one of them is communism. The other is our most ardent point of agreement but we only discuss it in knowing smiles at each other and the shyly understanding exchange of drinks and tomatoes, Etc. The little husband is polite and furious and is always trembling a little. There is a tremendous short story in the place for you or Christopher [also for Tennessee: "The Mattress by the Tomato Patch"], especially

*From *Tennessee Williams: Letters to Donald Windham, 1940–1965*, edited by Donald Windham, 1977. Reprinted by permission of Henry Holt & Co., Inc.

the woman on the raggedy mattress by the tomato patch with the great rocking days of California weaving in and out while she ages and laps up life with the tongue of a female bull.

[Via Aurora, Rome, Italy]
4/8/49

Dear Donnie:

I read your letter and story ["Rosebud"] this afternoon in the bar of the Inghilterra which is Frankie's social club and where we leave messages for each other such as "Gone to the movies. Meet you here at seven, Etc." Or "Too beautiful to stay indoors. I took the car." I was literally trembling with excitement over the story and it seemed like the best you had written up till about page 20: in fact till exactly that page, where he cannot get out of bed and starts dying. All the stuff about the drugstore, the motorcycle, the cold wet road and the rides and the girl and the incredibly perfect dialogue between them which is the best negro dialogue I've ever read—all of that is simply breathtaking in its simplicity and its rightness and its enormously real atmosphere. But I feel that somewhere around page twenty (as you probably feel yourself) that a wrong turn was taken, some kind of unnecessary, *evitable* turn, perhaps in an effort to make it more of what magazine editors think of as a short-story, and quite precipitately *you* went out of the story and it turned to writing instead of being. If you just chopped it off at page 20, you would still have a fine story, but I am sure you will find another way to end it, for it is, up to that point, even better than that other negro study, *The Warm Country*, in my opinion.

Excerpts from *Memoirs**

When I say that Hazel was probably much wiser about the sex scene than I, I am not altogether sure what I mean by that. For five or six years [beginning in 1927] she had been a loving girl-friend but the love was what the Victorians would describe as pure. Now this will come as a rather incredible bit of news, but Hazel permitted me to kiss her only twice a year on the lips, and that was at Christmas and on her birthday. In retrospect I wonder if she was actually what the shrinks call "frigid," or if she was being coquettishly demure to bring out a more aggressive attitude in me. I am inclined to think the latter is true, since I remember an afternoon in our very early teens when we visited the St. Louis art gallery, atop Art Hill in Forest Park; she headed straight for a room of ancient statuary containing *The Dying Gaul,* who was clad only in a fig leaf. Now take my word for this, it's the absolute truth: the fig leaf could be lifted and Hazel knew it. She lifted the fig leaf and asked me, "Is yours like this?"

She got no answer but a maidenly blush . . .

I have incorporated that little occurrence in one of my best short stories, published by the *New Yorker,* no less: its title was "Three Players of a Summer Game." The *New Yorker* cut it out of the story, that incident of the fig leaf, but I restored it when the story appeared in *Hard Candy* and I think rightly so, for the little girl in the story was based upon Hazel as a child—including the bit about the old car, the "electric." Mrs. Kramer, *grand'mère,* had an "electric" automobile and the pretentious old lady loved to sit in its square glass box tooling sedately among the more fashionable residential sections of the city. She doted on Hazel and she would sometimes allow Hazel to take me for rides. The electric only went at a speed of about twenty miles an hour, at the most. Later on the Kramers were to give Hazel a light green Packard, but that was quite a bit later . . .

I started writing at night [in 1934]. I would write and complete one story a week and mail it, as soon as I finished, to the distinguished story magazine called *Story*. It was the time when the young Saroyan had made a sensation in that magazine with "The Daring Young Man on the Flying Trapeze." At first the editors encouraged me with little personal notes of criticism. But soon I began to receive those dreadful "form" rejections.

I had Saturday afternoon off from my job at Continental. I had an unvarying regime for those lovely times of release. I would go to the Mercantile Library, far downtown in St. Louis, and read voraciously there; I would have a thirty-five-cent lunch at a pleasant little restaurant. And I would go home in a "service car"—to concentrate upon the week's short story. Of course all of Sunday was devoted to the story's completion. [. . .]

My work in the short-story form, then confined to weekends and spurred by strong coffee, was considerably better, and most of these stories are preserved in the archives of the University of Texas.

The onset of my cardiovascular condition occurred in the spring of 1934, and it is a condition which has remained with me ever since, in greatly varying degrees, sometimes not enough to draw my attention but other times sufficient to become an obsession.

The first dramatic onset of this condition, in the spring of 1934, was triggered by two things. First, the quite unexpected marriage of Hazel to a young man named Terrence McCabe, whom she had been dating at the University of Wisconsin. I felt as though the sky had fallen on me, and my reaction was to start working every evening on short stories, overcoming fatigue with black coffee.

One evening I was at work on a story titled "The Accent of a Coming Foot," perhaps the most mature short story that I undertook in that period. I had arrived at a climactic scene when I suddenly became aware that my heart was palpitating and skipping beats.

Having no means of sedation, not even a glass of wine, I did a crazy thing: I jumped up from the typewriter and rushed out onto the streets of University City. I walked faster and faster as though by this means I could outdistance the attack. I walked all the way from University City to Union Boulevard in St. Louis, expecting to drop dead at each step. It was an instinctual, an animalistic reaction, comparable to the crazed dash of a cat or dog struck by an automobile, racing round and round until it collapses, or to the awful wing-flopping run of a decapitated chicken.

This was in the middle of March. The trees along the streets were just beginning to bud, and somehow, looking up at those bits of spring-time green as I dashed along, had a gradually calming effect—and I turned toward home again with the palpitations subsiding. [. . .]

Shortly after I arrived in California [1943] to start employment in the movie-mill at MGM, I found what were to be ideal living-quarters in Santa Monica. It was a two-room apartment on Ocean Boulevard in a large frame building called The Palisades. It was managed by a fantastic woman, half gypsy, matrimonially shackled to an unpleasant little man who was withering with cancer. Her description, and her angry little husband's, are contained in one of my better short stories, "The Mattress by the Tomato Patch," and as for that summer, it was as golden as the later summers in Rome. [. . .]

Returning to St. Louis and the thirties.

Rose had a "serious" St. Louis beau. He was a junior executive at International, a young man of very personable appearance, social grace and apparently of great and unscrupulous ambition. For a few months he was quite attentive to Rose. They dated, I think, several times a week, they were almost going "steady," and Rose would tremble when the telephone rang, desperately hoping the call was for her and that it was from him.

This was while Dad's position as sales manager of Friedman-Shelby branch of International was still, if not ascendant, at least one of apparent permanence and continued promise.

But Dad was playing fast and loose with his position. He was continually alarming the "establishment" and International by his week-end habits. Significantly, he had not been elected to the "Board of Executives," despite the fact that he was the best and most popular sales manager of International, and the only one who delivered speeches. His speeches were eloquent—and pungent. He did not talk much about his success at oratory but I think it pleased him enormously. He got up there on the platform before the assembled salesmen much in the style of his political forebears running for high offices in East Tennessee.

"Now you boys and I all remember when we used to have to go around the corner and have a cigarette for breakfast . . ."

I mean like *that*—and they loved it.

But the scandal occurred—the episode at the all-night poker party [December 1936] at the Hotel Jefferson in which Dad lost an ear that had to be replaced by plastic surgery. This marked the beginning of the end for Dad's possible ascendancy to "the Board" at International.

It also marked the end of Rose's dates with her handsome and unscrupulously ambitious "beau," who no longer was a potential husband.

Her heart broke, then, and it was after that that the mysterious stomach trouble began.

But you don't know Miss Rose and you never will unless you come to know her through this "thing," for Laura of *Menagerie* was like Miss Rose only in her inescapable "difference," which that old female bobcat Amanda would not believe existed. And as I mentioned, you may know only a little bit more of her through "Portrait of a Girl in Glass."

Nowadays is, indeed, lit by lightning, a plague has stricken the moths, and Blanche has been "put away" . . .

Now I'll describe the lunatic events of last night [summer 1972]. I was scheduled to make two appearances at the New Theatre for my resumed "symposia" after the performance. The first was to be at 9:10, after the first Saturday evening show, the second at 12:10 after the second. I was intending, out of sheer madness, I suppose, to read my new story which I call my last one, "The Inventory at Fontana Belle."

Well, the audience at the early show last night was spared that experience by a seriocomic concomitance of misadventures.

I had a dinner date with Ruth Ford and Dotson Rader set up for 7:30. I was also, at the same hour, expecting my new friend, who was to join us for dinner. Dotson left messages for me to call Ruth. I did and it was apparent that she was the opposite of eager to keep the date. She said that Dotson was now incommunicado, locked in the little attic apartment, the eyrie, in which she has lately ensconced him. I told her that my friend and I would go to Billy Barnes's for a picnic on his terrace and that she and Dotson might join us if they felt so inclined. Well, they didn't. And I felt put down about that. And there were bad vibes in the air on Billy's penthouse terrace. There were several young male beauties present and they started disappearing together, as is the wont of the beautiful and young in the States. Billy became more and more distraught in appearance. Mr. Robert Fryer of the Ahmanson Theatre in Los Angeles, where they plan to revive *Streetcar* this winter in celebration of its twenty-fifth anniversary, did not help the situation. He seemed extremely cool and quite lacking in social charm and not at all amused by my efforts to be amusing. I began to feel strange, partly due to a vodka martini and two or three glasses of red wine.

It seems that I can't hold liquor anymore; consult my liver on that subject and perhaps also my brain.

Well, when it was time to go to the theatre for the so-called "symposium" I tripped over a garden hose on the terrace and fell flat on the pavement, suffering quite a few bloody abrasions. My young friend was truly solicitous and Billy was a bit hysterical-looking as antiseptics were applied by my friend to the cuts I'd suffered.

Actually we arrived at the theatre no more than two or three minutes late, but the audience was leaving. They had not been informed of my appearance. I supposed they thought that it would be one appearance too many. I don't know why I was so upset over this, it was a trivial matter. But Candy Darling's boy-friend had a car, a white convertible, waiting at the door and he offered to drive our party home. I said, "I've had it. Please deliver me to my hotel." On the way, Mr. Fryer suggested that I return to the theatre and read my short story to the second evening's audience, *before* the play. This struck, correctly or not, as a reflection upon my sanity and I flew into a blind rage at the man. I told him to shove his West Coast theatre and the announced revival of *Streetcar*, and I told him various other things no more polite, and then I asked to be let out of the car on a corner several blocks from the hotel. They wouldn't let me out but drove me to the hotel door. Billy and Fryer remained in the car, both speechless, and the three young men went up to my "Victorian Suite" at the Elysée to see that I didn't jump out the window, I guess. I soon got hold of myself, drinks were ordered up, my friend massaged my back and talked soothingly and affectionately to me until the phone rang and one of the producers said they had failed to announce my appearance inadvertently and they would pick me up at the Elysée for the midnight show.

It appears that I will do just about anything, now, to keep the show running, that is, short of a tango with a kangaroo partner. So I went. The curtain opened. There was a fair-sized house for midnight. I took a drink of wine and informed the audience that on this occasion I intended to amuse myself, primarily, by reading a story to them.

The eccentric aspects of the story—and eccentric is a mild term for it—didn't strike me until after. The reception of the reading was, I could say, perfunctory. Lately no one seems to laugh at my jokes on paper, perhaps they're too black, I don't know . . .

I then took the three kids to P. J. Clarke's eatery and we drank and ate and I then began to reflect more and more upon the frightening compulsive note of self-destruction in which I had been indulging myself lately.

My friend took one kid: another left alone in my hat, a Dobbs Western. I'd presented it to him—and another friend took me home. He's a nice kid and he is now asleep in the twin bed while I knock out this preposterous account of the night before . . .

Make of it what you will. I can make of it nothing but a sense of doom. [. . .]

Bowles [Paul, in December 1948] asked me to read a short story of his which became the title story for a collection published a year or two later. This story was "The Delicate Prey" and it shocked me. This seems odd, I know. And I think it was quite incomprehensible to Paul that I, who had published such stories as "Desire and the Black Masseur" should be shocked by "The Delicate Prey." I recognized it as a beautiful piece of prose but I advised him against its publication in the States. You see, my shocking stories had been published in expensive private editions by New Directions and never exhibited on a bookstore counter. [. . .]

But I have hardly touched at all upon my prose works aside from these memoirs, and I have written a goodly quantity of prose works, some of which I prefer to my plays.

Faye Dunaway is dedicated to the project of starring in a film based on my short story "The Yellow Bird." She has it on a record which she has played for me twice, a record that I made for Caedmon and that is a steady seller.

It seems to me that quite a few of my stories, as well as my one-acts, would provide interesting and profitable material for the contemporary cinema, if committed to such lovely hands as Miss Dunaway's. Or Jon Voight's. And to such cinematic masters of direction as Jack Clayton, who made of *The Great Gatsby* a film that even surpassed, I think, the novel by Scott Fitzgerald. [. . .]

After several nights without sleeping medication, I managed yesterday to score for two dozen Nembutals from a doctor and I made up for the nearly sleepless nights past by sleeping on a single yellow jacket, as Marion called them, from midnight until 9 A.M. I got up with the expectation that the long sleep would restore my energy for work, but the reverse was soon apparent.

My condition as I attempted to resume work on my story "Sabbatha and Solitude" [spring 1973] was next of kin to comatose, so I gave it up after the slight accomplishment of getting the pages into some kind of order.

About that story: it is a satire of sorts but I'm afraid it doesn't come off.

As a matter of fact, it is almost incoherent at points. Something is happening to me that's not very propitious and at a most inconvenient time, since I am very close, now, to the production of my last major work for the theatre. It may be that the imminence of this event has unnerved me. But haven't I always been unnerved?—So that excuse doesn't hold much water or even—what's less than water?—precipitation or dew?

Still, the story will someday come together. Given time enough, a piece of work does. And what's the hurry?

Part 3

THE CRITICS

Introduction

As I have noted a number of times throughout this study, critics in general have too often ignored Williams's short fiction in favor of his plays. This, however, does not mean that no criticism of his short fiction exists or that what does exist is without merit. On the contrary, interesting commentary on his short stories began to appear almost as soon as the stories themselves: that is, in the form of reviews. Since those early reviews, a number of insightful essays have been published.

Accordingly, reprinted here are two reviews and excerpts from two essays. One of the reviews, "Madness and Decay," by James Kelly, concerns Williams's first collection, *One Arm and Other Stories*. The other review, by Edmund White, addresses Williams's last collection, *Eight Mortal Ladies Possessed: A Book of Stories*. More extended treatment of Williams the short story writer is provided by William Peden in one of the earliest—and still one of the best—full essays on his work: "Mad Pilgrimage: The Short Stories of Tennessee Williams." An excerpt from a much later essay, Edward A. Sklepowich's "In Pursuit of the Lyric Quarry: The Image of the Homosexual in Tennessee Williams' Prose Fiction," concludes this section.

Madness and Decay
*James Kelly**

In three major Williams plays, one senses the compassion (proffered with moody bravura) and a rugged brand of élan in the manner of D. H. Lawrence. Certainly "Summer and Smoke," "The Glass Menagerie" and "A Streetcar Named Desire" are votes *for* life, no matter

*From the *New York Times Book Review*, 2 January 1955. Copyright © 1955 by the New York Times Co. Reprinted by permission.

how mixed up it sometimes gets. But compassion, or even healthy optimism, is nearly invisible in the lurid studies of perversion, madness and human decay covered by the one-act plays published prior to 1946 and by the eleven short subjects of the volume now before us (published first in 1948 as a limited edition).

Are these stories the recorded fantasies of a cynical young man with an overpowering urge to shock? Are they the preserved insights and memories of the author's squalid growing-up years which, on the other side of the coin, bring us the gentle beauty of the girl in "The Glass Menagerie"? Or can they be regarded as quick notes about the defeated, the directionless, mutilated, bereft, diseased people living in cribs and seedy boarding houses who are to figure in later mature work? Opinions will vary.

Styled like a Soutine painting, and faintly plotted, "One Arm and Other Stories" is held together chiefly by variations on one theme: "Desire is something that is made to occupy a larger space than that which is afforded by the individual being. . . . For the sins of the world are really only its partialities, its incompletions, and these are what sufferings must atone for." Q. E. D. To Mr. Williams, imagination, violence and surrender of self to others are simply the means for overcoming the guilt of incompletion.

In a Grand Guignol mood, "Desire and the Black Masseur" lovingly limns the relationship between a timid little man and a voracious Negro masseur which eventually does the little man's health no good at all. "One Arm," the forthright title story, features a mutilated male prostitute who begins to feel more aware of human dignity as he waits his turn in a prison deathhouse.

In a more identifiable vein, "Portrait of a Girl in Glass" tellingly reflects the dreamy adolescent girl who falls for a young man already spoken for; and two spirited collegiate stories, one about a co-ed and a boy who ardently pursue each other only to find that there's nothing there, the other about a poetic young couple who vividly experience the troublesome moods of pre-adulthood before going their separate ways.

Mr. Williams generally confines himself here to cruelty incarnate and its untrammeled expression. But these electrifying eleven are intimation enough of an interesting writer and a sensitive man. Queasiness aside, though, it'll be a real question for many onlookers whether in aiming low and on the inside the young pitcher hasn't forgotten to get it over the plate.

Eight Mortal Ladies Possessed
Edmund White*

As a writer of fiction, Tennessee Williams has two things going for him: he is never dull; and he knows how to ingratiate himself. If, in this collection of six new short stories, Williams is so captivating as a narrator, it is because he had invented a tone of voice that is both racy and genteel, that slyly alternates between juicy vulgarity and the mellifluous circumlocutions of a gentleman of the old school. Here's a specimen passage: "'Why, this old fart has gone *senile*.' Sabbatha shrieked to her audience of one, a young man whose Mediterranean aspects of character and appearance had magically survived his past ten years of sharing life with Sabbatha in her several retreats." The touches of cultivated diction ("aspects," "retreats") are amusing and are read (as they no doubt were written) with a smile.

At times the earthiness and the elegance come together in a paragraph that is peculiarly lovely and moving: "The morning light did not seem to care for the city, it seemed to be creeping into it and around it with understandable aversion. The city and the morning were embracing each other as if they'd been hired to perform an act of intimacy that was equally abhorrent to them both."

The important quality in Williams's style (as befits a playwright) is that it is *spoken;* you can imagine someone (an eloquent and mannered someone, of course) drawing you aside and telling you these sweet somethings. And because a conversational voice is recounting an incident of interest (usually of bizarre interest), Williams appears to write effortlessly. He never seems to fuss over exposition or scene-painting, no more than you would fuss if you were telling one of your best after-dinner stories.

Some of the pieces in this collection, however, might sound a good deal better if told over brandy and cigars. In fact, one, "Miss Coynte of Greene," is repellent in the cold light of the printed page. Miss Coynte is a Southern spinster, stifled by her nagging, ailing mother and beset by unfulfilled sexual longings. Once Miss Coynte shocks her mother to death (literally), she's free to sate her lust upon a succession of black men who all die (literally) from over-exertion. Granted, this does not make for dull reading, but it did strike me as sexist and racist

*From the *New York Times Book Review*, 6 October 1974. Copyright © 1974 by the New York Times Co. Reprinted by permission.

tripe, the product of a shallow if agitated imagination. The cliché characters (domineering mother, sex-crazed spinster, well-endowed bucks) could have been conceived by a Freudian analyst c. 1950—which is my way of saying that if the story weren't so silly it would be degrading to all concerned, author, reader and characters alike.

Fortunately the book is redeemed by one perfect tale, "Happy August the Tenth." Two middle-aged women, after living together for 10 years in New York, have a spat over their parrot, Lorita, and over the one woman's new circle of intellectual friends and the other woman's old circle of Sarah Lawrence school chums. The spat leads to dire threats, a break—and then to some sort of painful, tentative reconciliation. The story is sad and funny, terse but not so terse that it excludes the meandering feel of those spiteful, frightening, inconclusive events, those simultaneous monologues, called lovers' quarrels. The book should be read for this one tale alone; the last story, "Oriflamme," also merits attention.

If *Eight Mortal Ladies Possessed* is such an uneven collection, the fault may lie more with the American market for short fiction than it does with the author. The dreadful stories appeared originally in *Playboy* and *Playgirl*, which pay their contributors handsomely but which do have fairly strict editorial policies (for years *Playboy*, for instance, refused to publish a story in which the man comes off as a fool). The best Williams story, "Happy August the Tenth," originally appeared in *Antaeus*, a little magazine of merit that pays its writers, correspondingly, little. Like any other professional writer, Williams must want to be paid for his pains. "Happy August the Tenth," alas, has no sex interest to offer. Just beauty.

Mad Pilgrimage: The Short Stories of Tennessee Williams

*William H. Peden**

The short stories of Tennessee Williams (1914–), collected in *One Arm* (1948) and *Hard Candy* (1954),[1] have been largely overshadowed by the author's continuing success and notoriety as a playwright. In addition

*From *Studies in Short Fiction* 1 (Summer 1964). Reprinted by permission of *Studies in Short Fiction*.

to possessing special interest as occasionally being the first or early versions of characters and situations eventually developed into full-length plays,[2] Williams' stories are important in their own right and are at their best a permanent addition to the "sick" fiction of the forties and fifties.

The world of Williams' stories possesses considerable variety of method, yet at the same time it is as limited and circumscribed as Poe's, which in some ways it resembles. His stories are alike in their preoccupation with what one Williams character speaks of as the "sense of the enormous grotesquerie of the world."[3] They are permeated, too, with an air of profound melancholy, and iridescent with a faded beauty and corruption which recalls John Randolph's irreverent simile of a rotting mackerel in the moonlight, that "shines and stinks, and stinks and shines." Similar character types appear and reappear throughout Williams' stories: disillusioned or frustrated artists and intellectuals, sex-starved virgins or nymphomaniacs, faded gentlewomen and hypocritical clergymen, homosexuals and alcoholics, destructive women and likeable adolescents. Recurring motifs include decay, disease, abnormality, and above all *loss*, loss through the inexorable process of time and the subsequent fall from grace, a fall more often physiological than spiritual.

With almost no exceptions, Williams' people are adrift, unloved, and unwanted. Heredity often plays an important part in their alienation from "normal" or "approved" standards of conduct; their deterioration is hastened or precipitated by ironies of circumstance over which they have no control; they are exploited by their friends or family, or are slowly and often passively strangled by their own weaknesses and fears. "To love is to lose," Williams once wrote,[4] and in one way or other his characters are losers, not winners. To alter his statement to "To live is to lose" would suggest the common chord of his short fiction.

With few exceptions, Williams' best stories are those concerned with basically non-exceptional characters who are depicted with an understanding, sympathy, and compassion which makes ridiculous the comment that Williams, like Hardy, is a sadist who creates his people only to humiliate them. Perhaps the most memorable and the most moving of these stories is "Portrait of a Girl in Glass," with its depiction of the shy and introverted Laura, the "petals" of whose mind had simply closed with fear and who could make no "positive motion toward the world but stood at the edge of the water, so to speak, with feet that anticipated too much cold to move"[5] and who was to become the most appealing character in what still seems to be Williams' most moving play, *The Glass Menagerie*.

Characteristic, too, of this group of quiet, non-sensational stories is one of Williams's earliest, the first published under his own name, "The Field of Blue Children," an account of a transitory love affair between a young poet, Homer Stallcup, and an undergraduate sorority girl with minor literary aspirations. Homer, an "outsider," is encouraged by Myra, an "insider." They come together for a moment of love in a field of blue flowers, and subsequently drift apart. Myra marries an unexciting fraternity boy and slips into a humdrum marriage, and Homer simply fades out of her life.

Yet the memory of the incident in the field of blue flowers persists. Myra seldom feels "restless anymore" and abandons her verse writing; her "life seemed to be perfectly full without it." But she is impelled, one late spring evening several years after her marriage, to return to the scene of her first encounter with love.

> The field was exactly as she had remembered it. She walked quickly out among the flowers; then suddenly fell to her knees among them, sobbing. She cried for a long time . . . and then she rose to her feet and carefully brushed off her skirt and stockings. Now she felt perfectly calm and in possession of herself once more. She went back to the car. She knew that she would never do such a ridiculous thing as this again, for now she had left the last of her troublesome youth behind her.[6]

With its muted lyricism and its lowly diminishing cadences—"The whole field was covered with dancing blue flowers. There was a wind scudding through them and they broke before it in pale blue waves, sending up a soft whispering sound like the infinitely diminished crying of small children at play"[7]—the story reminds us that if Williams achieved fame as a playwright, he began his career as a dedicated and essentially traditional poet.

Equally memorable and depicted with similar understanding and compassion are the brother and sister of the presumably autobiographical story of adolescence and death, "The Resemblance between a Violin Case and a Coffin," which is a moving study of the loss of innocence and youth and beauty. Almost as impressive are Williams' characterizations of the awkward college students in "The Important Thing," and the actor protagonist of "The Vine," who is finally forced to accept the fact that he is washed up. His confrontation with the truth—all defenses broken, all illusions stripped from him—is one of the high marks in Williams' fiction.[8]

Perhaps the best of all of Williams' fictional creations is Brick Pollitt of "Three Players of a Summer Game." Delta planter, one-time famous Sewanee athlete, and dedicated alcoholic, Brick is eventually emasculated, spiritually and emotionally if not physically, by Margaret, one of the most destructive of Williams' predatory contemporary vampires ("It was as though she had her lips fastened to some invisible wound in his body through which drained out of him and flowed into her the assurance and vitality that he had owned before marriage.") By the end of the story, Brick is a pitiable ruin, driven through the streets in a Pierce Arrow by Margaret, "clothed and barbered with his usual immaculacy, so that he looked from some distance like the president of a good social fraternity in a gentleman's college of the South," but no longer a man, indeed no longer a human being, but a babbling and goggling wreck "sheepishly grinning and nodding," while Margaret gaily blows the "car's silver trumpet at every intersection," waving and calling to everybody "as if she were running for office," while Brick "nodded and grinned with senseless amiability behind her. It was exactly the way that some ancient conqueror, such as Caesar or Alexander the Great or Hannibal, might have led in chains through a captive city the prince of a state newly conquered."

Though he is unforgettably individualized, Brick Pollitt, like so many of Williams' people, is an effectively functioning symbol, in this case of waste, the waste of human grace and beauty and dignity. Such waste, and the attritions of time, are twin villains in Williams' view of the world. "Physical beauty," the narrator of "Three Players of a Summer Game" comments, is "of all human attributes the most incontinently used and wasted, as if whoever made it despised it, since it is made so often only to be disgraced by painful degrees and drawn through the streets in chains."[9]

These are Williams' great betrayers: waste and time together, they degrade and befoul, and are unconquerable.

A second group of Williams' short fiction tends to center around characters who are pathological or societal outcasts and rejects. Here again, Williams is concerned with the loss of beauty and grace, and with the attritions of time, along with an almost obsessive preoccupation with homosexuality, decay, and degradation. The best of these stories is "One Arm," set in the vicinity of New Orleans, which Williams knew so well and utilizes so effectively. Oliver Winemiller, apparently no kin to Alma Winemiller of *Summer and Smoke,* had been light-heavyweight boxing champion of the Pacific Fleet but subsequently loses his arm in an automobile accident. His degeneration and deterioration are rapid: Oliver becomes a male hustler, a notorious homosexual, and finally murders a wealthy man who had paid him to act in a "blue" movie. In jail, awaiting execution, Oliver finally feels the passion and desire which he had for so many years aroused in others. But it is of course too late, and Oliver goes to the chair lost and broken, incomplete and unfulfilled with "all his debts unpaid." Even in death, however, there is about Oliver something of the heroic, the beautiful. Unclaimed, Oliver's body becomes a cadaver in the medical school. The dissectors are "somewhat abashed by the body under their knives. It seemed intended for some more august purpose, to stand in a gallery of antique sculpture, touched only by light through stillness and contemplation, for it had the nobility of some broken Apollo that no one was likely to carve so purely again."[10]

There is similar pathos but very little similar nobility in the unhappy lives of most of Williams' other deviates. One can feel sorry for Edith Jelkes, the sex-starved spinster of "The Night of the Iguana," whom we are introduced to in Acapulco, where she is recuperating after having suffered "a sort of nervous breakdown" at the Mississippi Episcopal school where she had taught art. Like many of Williams' genteel no-longer-young ladies with a penchant for disaster, Edith is the victim of hereditary taints, and to that extent is only partially responsible for her actions.[11] Her dubious sexual triumph over a homosexual writer, however, is hardly cause for unlimited rejoicing. The writer himself, moreover, and his male companion, both of whom alternately attract and repel Edith, are essentially flat characters who fail to engage either our sympathy or dislike.

It is similarly difficult to sympathize with the two derelicts of "Two on a Party," one of the loneliest, saddest couples in recent literature. Billy is a onetime English instructor and Hollywood hackwriter who is currently a self-destroying egoist; Cora is a kindly lush with "none of that desire to manage and dominate which is a typically American perversion of the female nature."[12] Each of these whores is sympathetically observed and as convincing as a thunderstorm, and the terrible emptiness of their lives "on the road" is chillingly portrayed. But in the final analysis their story is as empty as their lives; Billy's only concern, apparently, is his fall from physiological grace and his morbid horror of his premature baldness, and Cora tends to fade into the background as the story progresses. Like the cancer-ridden protagonist of "The Mysteries of the Joy Rio" who is compelled to return to the seedy theatre where in the past he had enjoyed sexual delights with an elderly man,[13] Billy and Cora's destruction evokes little more than morbid horror.

Like "Two on a Party" and "The Mysteries of the Joy Rio," Williams' fantasies are memorable in their presentation of decay and disintegration, and are alive with that "Sense of the Awful" which Williams has called the "desperate black root of nearly all significant modern art."[14] For the most part, however, the fantasies seem the least successful of his short fiction; in them the depiction of what one Williams character calls the "mad pilgrimage of the flesh"[15] frequently approaches caricature or burlesque.

Probably the most successful and the best known of these symbolic excursions into the province of the grotesque, the Gothic, and the hallucinated is "Desire and the Black Masseur." From his childhood, Anthony Burns "had betrayed an instinct for being included in things that swallowed him up." Unloved, unlovable, and a passive leaf in the stream of life, Burns "loved to sit in the back rows of the movies where the darkness absorbed him gently . . . like a particle of food dissolving in a big hot mouth." One day he goes to a Turkish bath where he is administered to by a gigantic black masseur. He is attracted to the Negro and eventually "adores" the giant. In return the giant "loves" him, tortures him, and eventually devours him, flesh and splintered bones. As he drops the bones, "left over from Burns' atonement," into a lake, the black masseur thinks: "It is perfect . . . it is now completed!" Perfection and atonement, the story tells us, have gradually evolved out of the antitheses of love and hate, torture and delight. Meanwhile, the Negro, like some strange being above and beyond earthly passions, moves on to another city where he waits in a "white-curtained place, serenely conscious of fate bringing . . . another, to suffer atonement as it had been suffered by Burns . . . meantime, slowly, with barely a thought of so doing, the earth's whole population twisted and writhed beneath the manipulation of night's black fingers and the white ones of day with skeletons splintered and flesh reduced to pulp, as out of this unlikely problem, the answer, perfection, was slowly evolved through torture."[16]

Without raising the question of the author's purpose, or lack of it, "Desire and the Black Masseur" tends to fail because Williams makes no effort to bridge the gap between the specific framework of character, incident, time and place, and the allegorical, symbolic, or mythic. Though powerful in its Poe-like totality of effect of horror and madness, the story tends to fall apart as a self-contained piece of fiction. It is not fiction which suggests the universal in terms of the specific; it is undigested and indigestible allegory. Similarly "The Poet," the protagonist of which distills a liquor which makes the world change color, leads a life of benevolent anarchy, and it retreats into silence with an "incubus in his bosom, whose fierce little purplish knot of a head was butting against his ribs and whose limbs were kicking and squirming with convulsions."[17] "Yellow Bird," a burlesque written in a mocking, bantering tone fortunately absent from Williams' other stories, is similarly unsuccessful. It is difficult to find either amusement or edification in this study of the unmarried daughter of a Protestant minister, pushing thirty and mad for life and exitement, who begins by smoking in the attic and ends on "Monkey-Wrench Corner" of New Orleans' Vieux Carrée.

The humor in the story like "The Yellow Bird" is more often than not elephantine, the irony ponderous. The narrative method is similarly heavy-handed, involving such commentaries as "Now from this point on the story takes a strange turn that may be highly disagreeable to some readers, if any still hoped it was going to avoid the fantastic,"[18] which to most contemporary readers are likely to be as objectionable as those of Trollope. In spite of their defects, however, Williams' "blasted allegories"—the phrase, of course, is Hawthorne's—are a searing indictment of the cruelty and injustice of the world as the author sees it. Even at their least successful they have about them the same curious pathos that characterizes Williams' fiction in general.[19] Whatever his form, method, or mood the mad pilgrimage comes to the same dead end.

1. *One Arm* was originally published in a limited edition in 1948, and in a trade edition in 1954 (*One Arm and Other Stories* [Norfolk, Connecticut: New Directions]). *Hard Candy, A Book of Stories* was published in a limited edition

in 1954, also by New Directions. The quotations from *One Arm* are from the trade edition.

2. The relationships between the stories and the plays—between "Portrait of a Girl in Glass" and *The Glass Menagerie*, "The Yellow Bird" and *Summer and Smoke*, "Three Players of a Summer Game" and *Cat on a Hot Tin Roof*, and "Night of the Iguana" and the play of the same name—are commented on briefly by Benjamin Nelson in *Tennessee Williams. The Man and His Work* (New York, 1961), 185. They are not discussed in any recent critical biographies, Signi Lenea Falk's *Tennessee Williams* (New York, 1961) or Nancy Tischler's *Tennessee Williams: Rebellious Puritan* (New York, 1961). The Nelson biography contains a good discussion of Williams' short stories, pp. 185–97.

3. "The Night of the Iguana," *One Arm*, p. 188.

4. In Williams' Foreword to *Sweet Bird of Youth* (Norfolk, Connecticut, 1959), p. viii.

5. "Portrait of a Girl in Glass," *One Arm*, p. 97.

6. "The Field of Blue Children," *One Arm*, p. 166.

7. Ibid., p. 164.

8. "The Resemblance between a Violin Case and a Coffin" and "The Vine" are in *Hard Candy*; "The Important Thing" is in *One Arm*.

9. "Three Players of a Summer Game," *Hard Candy*, pp. 14, 43, 44.

10. "One Arm," *One Arm*, p. 29.

11. "She belonged to an historical Southern family of great but now moribund vitality whose later generations had tended to split into two antithetical types, one in which the libido was pathologically distended and another in which it would seem to be all but dried up. The households were turbulently split and so, fairly often, were the personalities of their inmates. There had been an efflorescence among them of nervous talents and sickness, of drunkards and poets, gifted artists and sexual degenerates, together with fanatically proper and squeamish old ladies of both sexes who were condemned to live beneath the same roof with relatives whom they could only regard as monsters." ("The Night of the Iguana," *One Arm*, p. 170.)

12. "Two on a Party," *Hard Candy*, p. 57.

13. "The Mysteries of the Joy Rio" is in *Hard Candy*.

14. Tennessee Williams, "Preface," Carson McCullers, *Reflections of a Golden Eye* (Norfolk, Connecticut, 1940).

15. "The Malediction," *One Arm*, p. 55.

16. "Desire and the Black Masseur," *One Arm*, pp. 83, 93, 94.

17. "The Poet," *One Arm*, pp. 64–65.

18. "The Yellow Bird," *One Arm*, p. 209.

19. Some of these comments originally appeared in my "Broken and Blue Dreams," *Saturday Review* (Jan. 5, 1955), pp. 11–12.

In Pursuit of the Lyric Quarry: The Image of the Homosexual in Tennessee Williams's Prose Fiction

Edward A. Sklepowich*

Williams' so-called "decadent" vision and his preoccupation with lone-liness, evasion, role-playing, wastage, sexual reluctance and sexual ex-cess are in many instances functions of a homosexual sensibility which has been evolving steadily in the more than quarter century since the publication of *One Arm and Other Stories* [1948]. In this period Williams' treatment of homosexuality has undergone significant changes, moving from a mystical to a more social perspective, a personal, if fictional microcosm of the wider cultural demystification of homosexuality. The characteristic homosexuals of Williams' early fiction and of plays such as *Camino Real* and *Suddenly Last Summer* are lonely men, frequently vagabonds, with the aura of the demigod, saint, repentant sinner, or poète maudit. In *Moise* the homosexual is an individual with a more identifiable and "realistic" relationship to his surrounding social and historical milieus. Briefly stated, then, Williams' homosexual has moved from the mythic to the real.

In "One Arm," the title story of his first collection, Williams uses the figure of the male hustler as a vehicle for a statement on the tran-scendence of mundanity, alienation, and loneliness through unconven-tional sexuality. Less about the homosexual sensibility or underworld than about the power of sexuality itself, a power whose object—woman, man, or self—is of relatively minor importance, the tale re-cords the transformation of the one-armed Ollie Winemiller from hustler to pagan love god. Ollie, a blond youth of twenty evocative of a "broken statue of Apollo" (p. 7), appears to be caught in forces be-yond his conscious control. One of Williams' fugitive kind, Ollie, the "center of his being" (p. 9) dislocated after the loss of his arm, drifts into a life of hustling which allows him to capitalize on his broken beauty while enacting the self-destructive impulse he only half-recog-nizes within himself. His rootless existence is ended when he murders

*From *Tennessee Williams: A Tribute*, edited by Jack Tharpe, © 1977 by the University of Mississippi Press. Reprinted by permission of the University of Mississippi Press.

Edward A. Sklepowich

one of his "tricks" in an act of almost Camusian violence and finds himself on death row.

While awaiting execution, however, Ollie undergoes a strange and beautiful alteration. Because of the considerable publicity generated about this "baby-faced killer" (p. 21), many of his former contacts write him touching letters, frequently with money enclosed, describing the profound influence he has had on them. Something about their fleeting contact with this hustler which transcended the physical has haunted their minds ever since, and they face life as altered individuals. These men are responding not only to his beauty and grace but also to that engaging "charm of the defeated" (p. 13) that has seemed to surround him like the aura of a saint, of some remote, posturing Saint Sebastian. These letters from his disciples are instrumental in the reestablishment of Ollie's pride; his self-conception begins to change and to unfold like an opening flower. Previously unmoved by either homosexual or heterosexual sex, in the characteristically self-assured manner of the hustler, Ollie now masturbates with a sense of joyless wonder, his masturbatory acts resembling the understandably selfish rites of a god. Through autoeroticism and fantasy Ollie reawakens his emotional life, but the rediscovery of his "rainbows of the flesh" (p. 19) torments as much as it enraptures him because his confinement and impending death impose obvious limits on his behavior and continued development. Ollie, now anguished by the reanimated sense of his own beauty and grace, finally suffers his death by electrocution with the letters clasped erotically between his thighs.

An episode during the terminal days of Ollie's life clarifies many of the values of the story and draws additional attention to its homosexual aspects. On a visit of charity a young Lutheran minister attempts to console Ollie. Alone with the condemned man, the minister is reminded, by Ollie's lithe, bronzed body, of the golden panther of his erotic dream life and becomes totally confused as he wipes the amber sweat from Ollie's limbs, fighting desperately against the gravity of his beauty. When Ollie, after rejecting the minister's puerile religious consolations, asks him to rub his back, dropping his shorts more seductively and confessing his loneliness and emotional frustration, the minister calls frantically for the guard to rescue him from temptation.

The minister, too fettered by concepts imposed by society and self to accept affection and love in unfamiliar guise, cannot even comprehend Ollie's fervent self-revelations. Also, the minister's latent homosexuality is not what contorts him, but rather his unwillingness to

125

face the truth of his homosexuality, much like Brick in *Cat on a Hot Tin Roof*. The true prison is that of self, and the minister is unable to break out as Ollie is gradually learning—or relearning—to do. That the only repository of grace and perhaps of salvation in the story is a hustler is most significant. Ollie becomes a force of good in a world usually too blind or too fearful to recognize, acknowledge, or accept that good when its epiphany occurs in an unorthodox form or context. The medical students who dissect Ollie's body after death marvel at its physical beauty and feel it was "intended for some more august purpose" (p. 29), but the true, transformative mysteries of love and emotion in which Ollie has participated elude them. Although the transformation might not have been completed within Ollie, he has come closer than most to a truth of religious dimensions.

A similar situation is depicted in the Italian film *Teorema* (1967) by the homosexual director Pasolini. In this haunting film a beautiful young man appears in the lives of a bourgeois family, makes love in turn to the mother, daughter, father, and son, and then vanishes, having infused his sexual partners with a grace and an understanding of such intensity that they approach the mysterious and the inexplicable. In the end Ollie, too, appears to transcend sexual categories much as did the classical Greek and Roman gods. One critic, in fact, refers to the "mystical quality of giving which glorifies such personalities."[1] Beautiful yet mutilated, guilty yet innocent, wise yet untutored, dead yet living in the memories of his former contacts, Ollie is multiple and paradoxical, the personification of a secular transcendence.

"Desire and the Black Masseur" (1948), the next of Williams' stories to deal with sexuality of an ambiguous nature, presents its own ritual of love, death, and redemption, yet in a more distorted and unrealistic manner. This tale has earned considerable notoriety because of its bizarre subject matter. Homosexual sadomasochism and cannibalism are, Edmund Fuller believes, more the province of clinical case studies than of the short story.[2] "Desire and the Black Masseur" is the account of Anthony Burns's tortured search for security. Obsessed with the desire to be swallowed and engulfed as compensation for his innate insecurity, Burns first seeks out movie houses whose film images wash over him and lull him like some therapeutic, amniotic bath. However, Burns is not long in finding the ultimate arena for his obsession, a massage parlor with much of the mystery and eroticism of Madame Irma's house of illusions in Genêt's *The Balcony*. While being pummeled by a massive black masseur, Burns discovers his own masochism as waves of pleasure, triggered by the acute pain, rush over him.

Through deft rhetorical manipulations, Burns's masochism, like Ollie's hustling or Sebastian Venable's liaisons, assumes a significance beyond the ordinary and the mundane. Burns's obsession is something greater than himself, occupying, like all desire, "a larger space than that which is afforded by the individual being" (*One Arm*, p. 84). Williams presents us with a parable similar to the one Pauline Réage was to explore later in *Story of O.:* the masochist's transcendence of his limited circumstances and his accomplishment of a religious atonement by eremitically rejecting the good things of this life and submitting to authority from a god-surrogate. Williams' conclusion, like Réage's alternative ending, implies that the logical extreme of the masochistic psychology is death, in this instance one of a particularly redemptive kind, for, in the isolated quarters of the masseur, Burns allows himself to be pummeled to death; and, in a final macabre twist, his body is ritualistically consumed by the masseur. The religious significance Williams wishes to give to his story is made clear by his counterpointing of Burns's destruction with the Easter celebration or "massive atonement" (p. 92) taking place simultaneously at a nearby church. The last vestiges of Burns in the story are his white bones, dropped into the river by the masseur, bones reminiscent of those of the Phoenician sailor in *The Waste Land*, picked clean and purified beneath the waves. Burns's death, as is emphasized at the end, is a "perfection . . . slowly evolved through torture" (p. 94).

The sadomasochistic ritual merits some further comment. The chilling appropriateness of the sadomasochistic scenario, as enacted by Burns and the masseur, results from its combination of the aesthetic, the violent, and the religious. As the narrator says, art, violence, and atonement are three ways of compensating for the kind of incompletion Burns shares with alienated modern man. Atonement, described as "surrender of self to violent treatment by others" (p. 85), is motivated by the desire to absolve onself of some dimly understood but profoundly disturbing guilt. Like O., who considers the physical, psychological, and emotional abuse of herself as "the very redemption of her sins,"[3] Burns suffers violence as a mode of self-knowledge, pleasure, and exaltation. His masochistic surrender to the masseur indicates with what intensity the Williams character shuns isolation and desires interaction with another, even if it is violent and destructive. The violence, however, is controlled and regulated in almost ludic fashion, with the interaction between Burns and the masseur suggestive of a ritual with its own lovely form and content. This is ceremonial rather than haphazard violence, as is Mishima's gladiatorial blood-theater in *Confessions of a Mask* in which beautiful young men are killed with much overflow of blood but "with all due ceremony."[4]

The implications of this tale for Williams' evolving theme of homosexuality are intriguing, if not heavily conclusive. Might Williams be obliquely suggesting some parallels between the erotic fascination with pain and death and the homosexual sensibility, as do Genêt and Mishima? Or perhaps he is intimating that what is fulfilment for the homosexual is actually death to this world with its restrictive social and religious standards. Possibly he is telling us that it is time for a new concept of Christ, for yet another version of the "man who died," except this time the version will be his, and not Lawrence's. Certainly in his death Burns suggests, perhaps comes close to parodying, the Christ of the Last Supper and the Passion.[5] At any rate, "Desire and the Black Masseur" is another of Williams' early stories which uses ambiguous or unconventional sexuality as a vehicle for a statement of mythic or religious import. The deaths of Ollie, Burns, and Sebastian are more like the deaths of Orpheus, Saint Sebastian, and Christ than those of more typical men.

1. Signi Lenea Falk, *Tennessee Williams* (New York: Twayne Publications, 1961), 41.

2. Edmund Fuller, *Man in Modern Fiction* (New York: Random House, 1949), p. 70.

3. Pauline Réage, *Story of O.* (New York: Grove Press, 1965), p. 93.

4. Yukio Mishima, *Confessions of a Mask*, trans. from the Japanese by Meredith Weatherby (New York: New Directions, 1958), pp. 92–3.

5. Cf. Nancy M. Tischler, *Tennessee Williams* (New York: Citadel Press, 1961), p. 259, who refers to the similarities between the action of the story and the sacrifice of the Mass but does not suggest that parody might be involved.

Chronology

1907   Cornelius Coffin Williams and Edwina Estelle Dakin (Tennessee Williams's parents) marry.

1909   Sister, Rose Isabel, born.

1911   Thomas Lanier (Tennessee) Williams born, 26 March, Columbus, Georgia.

1913–1915   Lives with mother and grandparents in Nashville, Tennessee.

1915–1918   Lives with mother and grandparents in Clarksdale, Mississippi.

1917   Kept out of first grade due to illness.

1918   Family moves to St. Louis, Missouri. Williams enters Eugene Field Elementary School.

1919   Brother, Walter Dakin, born.

1922   Debacle at Rose's violin recital (see "The Resemblance between a Violin Case and a Coffin").

1924   Short story, "A Great Tale Told at Katrina's Party," published in junior high paper, *Junior Life*.

1927   Wins $5 prize for letter to *Smart Set* in reply to question, "Can a good wife be a good sport?"

1928   "The Vengeance of Nitocris" published in *Weird Tales*, Williams's first short story in a national magazine. With grandfather, sees *Showboat* on Broadway.

1929   Graduates from University City High School, 53rd in class of 83. Enters University of Missouri at Columbia. Joins Alpha Tau Omega fraternity.

1930   Play, "Beauty Is the Word," listed among honorable mention in Dramatic Arts Club (Columbia, Missouri) contest. Short story, "A Lady's Beaded Bag," appears in University of Missouri literary magazine.

1931   Sees, and is moved by, a production of Ibsen's *Ghosts*.

1932   Withdraws from University of Missouri.

1934–1935   Works off and on for International Shoe Company, St. Louis.

1935   Suffers physical/emotional breakdown and resigns from International Shoe. Stays for a few months with grandparents in Memphis. A play, "Cairo, Shanghai, Bombay," coauthored with Bernice Dorothy Shapiro, produced by amateur group in Memphis. Enrolls in Washington University, St. Louis. "Stella for Star" wins first prize ($10) in the Winifred Irwin short story contest, sponsored by the St. Louis Writers Guild.

1936   Play, "The Magic Tower," wins first prize in Webster Groves Theatre Guild contest. Short story, "Twenty-seven Wagons Full of Cotton," published in *Manuscript.*

1937   Rose begins treatment at state asylum in Farmington, Missouri (January). Williams enters University of Iowa, has brief affair with coed. Surgery (prefrontal lobotomy) performed on Rose (fall).

1938   Graduates with B.A. in English from University of Iowa. Adopts "Tennessee" as preferred name. Travels to Chicago, then New Orleans, in search of work. Much of remainder of life spent largely in transit.

1939   Wins special $100 award from Group Theatre in New York for several one-act plays. Acquires agent, Audrey Wood. Visits D. H. Lawrence's widow in Taos, New Mexico. Arrives in New York City. Rockefeller Foundation awards $1000 grant.

1940   Play, *Battle of Angels,* opens in Boston.

1942   Play, *This Property Is Condemned,* performed at the New School, New York City.

1943   Becomes screenwriter in Hollywood. Fired a few months later.

1944   Play, *The Glass Menagerie,* opens in Chicago.

1946   Meets and becomes lifelong friends with Carson McCullers.

1947   Meets Frank Merlo, for whom Williams will develop the longest and deepest romantic attachment of his life.

1948   First short story collection, *One Arm and Other Stories*, published in limited edition by New Directions. Wins Pulitzer Prize for *A Streetcar Named Desire*.

1950   Buys house in Key West, which will become the closest thing to a permanent home for Williams. Wins Tony Award for *The Rose Tattoo*. Short story "The Resemblance between a Violin Case and a Coffin," published in *Flair*.

1952   Elected—along with Carson McCullers, Newton Arvin, Eudora Welty, Louise Bogan, and Jacques Barzun—to lifetime membership in the National Institute of Arts and Letters. Short story "Three Players of a Summer Game," published in the *New Yorker*.

1954   *Hard Candy: A Book of Stories* published by New Directions.

1955   Grandfather, who had lived with Williams off and on much of his later years, dies at age 97. Receives Pulitzer Prize for *Cat on a Hot Tin Roof*.

1956   Movie *Baby Doll*, based on several earlier Williams works—opens to outrage from religious and family groups.

1957   Father dies at age 77. Williams begins psychotherapy with Dr. Laurence S. Kubie in New York City.

1961   Relationship with Frank Merlo begins to sour. *The Night of the Iguana*, generally considered Williams's last great play, opens in New York.

1962   Makes cover of *Time* (9 March). Elected to lifetime fellowship in the American Academy of Arts and Letters.

1963   Frank Merlo dies. Drug dependency worsens.

1964   Begins romantic relationship with William Glavin.

1967   *The Knightly Quest: A Novel and Four Short Stories* published by New Directions.

1969   Converts to Catholicism. Receives honorary doctorate from the University of Missouri—Columbia. Admitted to Barnes Hospital, St. Louis, for treatment of drug abuse (September); has two heart attacks while there.

1970   Longtime friend and traveling companion, Marion Black Vaccaro, dies.

1971   Ends professional relationship with agent Audrey Wood. Bill Barnes becomes new agent.

1974   *Eight Mortal Ladies Possessed: A Book of Stories* published by New Directions.

1975   *Memoirs* published.

1978   *Androgyne, Mon Amor,* collection of poetry, published.

1980   *Clothes for a Summer Hotel,* last Broadway play, opens and closes. Mother dies, 1 June. Medal of Freedom presented at White House by President Carter.

1981   Selected, along with Harold Pinter, for third annual Common Wealth Award.

1982   *A House Not Meant to Stand,* Williams's last play, opens in Chicago. Williams's last public appearance, reading at a New York YMHA.

1983   Dies of drug overdose/respiratory blockage at Élysée Hotel, New York City, 24 February.

Bibliography

Primary Sources

Collections

One Arm and Other Stories. New York: New Directions, 1948. Includes: "One Arm," "The Malediction," "The Poet," "Chronicle of a Demise," "Desire and the Black Masseur," "Portrait of a Girl in Glass," "The Important Thing," "The Angel in the Alcove," "The Field of Blue Children," "The Night of the Iguana," "The Yellow Bird."

Hard Candy: A Book of Stories. New York: New Directions, 1954. Includes: "Three Players of a Summer Game," "Two on a Party," "The Resemblance between a Violin Case and a Coffin," "Hard Candy," "Rubio y Morena," "The Mattress by the Tomato Patch," "The Coming of Something to the Widow Holly," "The Vine," "The Mysteries of the Joy Rio."

Three Players of a Summer Game and Other Stories. Harmondsworth, England: Penguin Books, 1965. Includes: "Three Players of a Summer Game," "The Important Thing," "One Arm," "Portrait of a Girl in Glass," "The Coming of Something to the Widow Holly," "Two on a Party," "The Yellow Bird," "The Field of Blue Children," "The Malediction," "The Angel in the Alcove," "The Resemblance between a Violin Case and a Coffin," "The Night of the Iguana."

The Knightly Quest and Other Stories. New York: New Directions, 1966. Includes: "The Knightly Quest," "Mama's Old Stucco House," "Man Bring This Up Road," "The Kingdom of Earth," "Grand."

The Knightly Quest: A Novella and Twelve Short Stories. London: Secker and Warburg, 1968. Includes: "The Knightly Quest," "The Poet," "Chronicle of a Demise," "Desire and the Black Masseur," "Hard Candy," "Rubio y Morena," "The Mattress by the Tomato Patch," "The Vine," "The Mysteries of the Joy Rio," "Mama's Old Stucco House," "Man Bring This Up Road," "The Kingdom of Earth," "Grand."

Eight Mortal Ladies Possessed: A Book of Stories. New York: New Directions, 1974. Includes: "Happy August the Tenth," "The Inventory of the Fontana Bella," "Miss Coynte of Greene," "Sabbatha and Solitude," "Completed," "Oriflamme."

Reprints in Anthologies

"The Coming of Something to the Widow Holly." In *New Directions in Prose and Poetry*, no. 14, 194–201, edited by James Laughlin. New York: New Directions, 1953.

"Desire and the Black Masseur." In *New Directions in Prose and Poetry*, no. 10, 239–46, edited by James Laughlin. New York: New Directions, 1948.

"The Field of Blue Children." In *Twenty-three Modern Stories*, 92–102, edited by Barbara Howes. New York: Vintage, 1963.

"Happy August the Tenth." In *The Best American Short Stories, 1973*, 276–88, edited by Martha Foley. Boston: Houghton Mifflin, 1973.

"The Resemblance between a Violin Case and a Coffin." In *The Best American Short Stories, 1951*, 338–50, edited by Martha Foley. Boston: Houghton Mifflin, 1951.

"Rubio y Morena." In *New Directions in Prose and Poetry*, no. 11, 459–71, edited by James Laughlin. New York: New Directions, 1949.

"Three Players of a Summer Game." In *The Best American Short Stories, 1953*, 363–83, edited by Martha Foley. Boston: Houghton Mifflin, 1953.

"Two on a Party." In *The Other Persuasion: An Anthology of Short Fiction about Gay Men and Women*, 175–94, edited by Seymour Kleinberg, 1977.

"The Yellow Bird." In *Stories of the Modern South*, 408–15, edited by Benjamin Forkner and Patrick Samway. New York: Bantam, 1978.

Secondary Sources

Books and Parts of Books

Bradbury, John M. *Renaissance in the South: A Critical History of the Literature, 1920–1960*, 192–95. Chapel Hill: University of North Carolina Press, 1963.

Falk, Signi Lenea. *Tennessee Williams*. Boston: Twayne, 1978.

Fayard, Jeanne. *Tennessee Williams*. Paris: Seghers, 1972.

Fedder, Norman J. *The Influence of D. H. Lawrence on Tennessee Williams*. The Hague: Mouton, 1966.

Gray, Richard. *The Literature of Memory: Modern Writers of the American South*. Baltimore: Johns Hopkins University Press, 1977. 258–60.

Gunn, Drewey Wayne. *Tennessee Williams: A Bibliography*. Metuchen, New Jersey: Scarecrow Press, 1980.

Hauptmann, Robert. *The Pathological Vision: Jean Genet, Louis-Ferdinand Céline, and Tennessee Williams*. New York: Lang, 1984.

Jackson, Esther Merle. *The Broken World of Tennessee Williams*. Madison: University of Wisconsin Press, 1965.

Jauslin, Christian. *Tennessee Williams*. Hannover: Friedrich, 1969.
Londré, Felicia Hardison. *Tennessee Williams*. New York: Ungar, 1979.
McCann, John S. *The Critical Reputation of Tennessee Williams: A Reference Guide*. Boston: G. K. Hall, 1983.
Maxwell, Gilbert. *Tennessee Williams and Friends*. Cleveland: World Publishing, 1965.
Nelson, Benjamin. *Tennessee Williams*. New York: Astor-Havor, 1961.
————. *Tennessee Williams: The Man and His Work*. New York: Ivan Obolensky, 1961.
Peterson, Carol. *Tennessee Williams*. Berlin: Colloquium, 1975.
Rader, Dotson. *Tennessee: Cry of the Heart*. Garden City, New York: Doubleday, 1985.
Ramaswamy, S. "The Short Stories of Tennessee Williams." In *Indian Studies in American Fiction*, 263–85, edited by M. K. Naih et al. Delhi: Macmillan India, 1974.
Rasky, Harry. *Tennessee Williams: A Portrait in Laughter and Lamentation*. New York: Dodd, Mead, 1986.
Rogers, Ingrid. *Tennessee Williams: A Moralist's Answer to the Perils of Life*. European University Studies, Anglo-Saxon Language and Literature Series. New York: Lang, 1976.
Steen, Mike. *A Look at Tennessee Williams*. New York: Hawthorn, 1969.
Tennessee Williams. Edited by Harold Bloom. Modern Critical Views—Modern American Series. Edgemont, Pennsylvania: Chelsea House, 1986.
Tennessee Williams. Edited by Margaret A. Van Antwerp and Sally Johns. Detroit: Gale, 1984.
Tennessee Williams: A Collection of Critical Essays. Edited by Stephen S. Stanton. Englewood Cliffs, New Jersey: Prentice-Hall, 1977.
Tennessee Williams: A Tribute. Edited by Jac Tharpe. Jackson: University Press of Mississippi, 1977.
Theim, Willy H. *Tennessee Williams*. Dusseldorf: W. Girardet, 1956.
Tischler, Nancy Marie. *Tennessee Williams*. Austin, Texas: Steck-Vaughn, 1969.
————. *Tennessee Williams: Rebellious Puritan*. New York: Citadel Press, 1961.
Weales, Gerald C. *Tennessee Williams*. University of Minnesota Pamphlets on American Writers. Minneapolis: University of Minnesota Press, 1965.
Williams, Edwina Dakin, as told to Lucy Freeman. *Remember Me to Tom*. New York: Putnam's, 1963.
The World of Tennessee Williams. Edited by Richard F. Leavitt. New York: Putnam's, 1978.

Articles

Adler, Jacob H. "Williams' Eight Ladies." Review of *Eight Mortal Ladies Possessed. Southern Literary Journal* 8 (Fall 1975): 165–69.

Bibliography

Adler, Thomas P., Judith Hersh Clark, and Lyle Taylor. "Tennessee Williams in the Seventies: A Checklist." *Tennessee Williams Newsletter* 2 (1980): 24–29.

Annan, Gabriele. "Eros Denied." Review of *Eight Mortal Ladies Possessed*. *Times Literary Supplement*, 1 Aug. 1975, 865.

Atkinson, Brooks. "A Theater of Life." Review of *The Knightly Quest*. *Saturday Review* 50 (25 Feb. 1967): 53.

Bailey, Paul. "Dead Stork." Review of *Eight Mortal Ladies Possessed*. *New Statesman* 90 (4 July 1975): 29–30.

Blackwell, Louise. "Tennessee Williams and the Predicament of Women." *South Atlantic Bulletin* 35 (1970): 9–14.

Brown, Cecil. "Interview with Tennessee Williams." *Partisan Review* 45 (1978): 276–305.

Clayton, John S. "The Sister Figure in the Works of Tennessee Williams." *Carolina Quarterly* 11 (Summer 1960): 47–60.

Da Ponte, Durant. "Tennessee Williams' Gallery of Feminine Characters." *Tennessee Studies in Literature* 10 (1965): 7–26.

Derounian, Kathryn Zabelle. "'The Kingdom of Earth' and *The Kingdom of Earth (The Seven Descents of Myrtle):* Tennessee Williams' Parody." *University of Mississippi Studies in English* 4 (1983): 150–58.

Engle, Paul. "Locomotive Named Reality." Review of *One Arm*. *New Republic* 132 (24 Jan. 1955): 26–27.

Fritscher, John J. "Some Attitudes and a Posture: Religious Metaphor and Ritual in Tennessee Williams' Query of the American God." *Modern Drama* (Sept. 1970): 201–15.

Gaines, Ervin J. Review of *The Knightly Quest: A Novella and Four Short Stories*. *Library Journal* 92 (15 Apr. 1967): 1647.

Gorowa, Krishna. "The Fire Symbol in Tennessee Williams." *Literary Half-Yearly* 8 (1967): 57–73.

Grande, Luke M. "Metaphysics of Alienation in Tennessee Williams' Short Stories." *Drama Critique* 4 (Nov. 1961): 118–22.

Hurley, Paul J. "Williams' 'Desire and the Black Masseur': An Analysis." *Studies in Short Fiction* 2 (Fall 1964): 51–55.

Kelly, James. "Madness and Decay." Review of *One Arm*. *New York Times Book Review*, 2 Jan. 1955, 5.

Malin, Irvin. Review of *Eight Mortal Ladies Possessed*. *New Republic* 171 (14 Sept. 1974): 27–28.

Peden, William H. "Broken Apollos and Blasted Dreams." Review of *One Arm and Other Stories*. *Saturday Review* 38 (8 Jan. 1955): 11–12.

———. "Mad Pilgrimage: The Short Stories of Tennessee Williams." *Studies in Short Fiction* 1 (1964): 243–50.

———. "The Recent American Short Story." Review of *Eight Mortal Ladies Possessed*. *Sewanee Review* 82 (1974): 712–29.

Phillips, Robert. "Evidence for Fame." Review of the *Collected Stories*. *Commonweal* 113 (14 Mar. 1986): 156.

———. Review of *Eight Mortal Ladies Possessed*. *Commonweal* 102 (11 Apr. 1975): 55.

Portis, Rowe. Review of *Eight Mortal Ladies Possessed*. *Library Journal* 99 (1 Apr. 1974): 1060–61.

Presley, Delma E. "Tennessee Williams: Twenty-five Years of Criticism." *Bulletin of Bibliography* 30 (Jan./Mar. 1973): 21–29.

Price, Reynolds. "His Battle Cry Was 'Valor'!" Review of the *Collected Stories*. *New York Times Book Review*, 1 Dec. 1985, 11.

Quinn, J. J. Review of *The Knightly Quest*. *Best Sellers* 26 (1967): 440.

Reck, Tom S. "The Short Stories of Tennessee Williams: Nucleus for His Drama." *Tennessee Studies in Literature* 16 (1971): 141–54.

Review of *Eight Mortal Ladies Possessed*. *Choice* 11 (Jan. 1975): 1636.

Review of *The Knightly Quest*. *Critic* 25 (June/July 1967): 90.

Rorem, Ned. "Tennessee Now and Then." Review of *Eight Mortal Ladies Possessed*. *Saturday Review/World* 2 (21 Sept. 1974): 24–26. Reprinted in *London Magazine* (June–July 1975): 68–74.

Roth, Robert. Review of *One Arm*. *Chicago Review* 9 (Summer 1955): 86–94.

Tischler, Nancy Marie. Review of the *Collected Stories*. *Choice* 23 (1986): 1068.

Vidal, Gore. "Selected Memories of the Glorious Bird and the Golden Age." *New York Review of Books*, 5 Feb. 1976, 13–18.

Vogel, Carl. Review of the *Collected Stories*. *Library Journal* 110 (15 Oct. 1985): 104.

Von Szeliski, John. "Tennessee Williams and the Tragedy of Sensitivity." *Western Humanities Review* 20 (1966): 203–11.

Wakeman, John. "Story Time." Review of *The Knightly Quest*. *New York Times Book Review*, 2 Apr. 1967, 4.

White, Edmund. "Tennessee Williams' Six Short Stories." Review of *Eight Mortal Ladies Possessed*. *New York Times Book Review*, 6 Oct. 1974, 14.

Zimmerman, Paul D. "Offstage Voices." Review of *The Knightly Quest*. *Newsweek* 69 (27 Feb. 1967): 92.

Index

Index

About the Author

Dennis Vannatta is professor of English at the University of Arkansas at Little Rock, where he specializes in contemporary literature and the short story. He received his Ph. D. in English from the University of Missouri-Columbia in 1978 and has published three books: *Nathanael West: An Annotated Bibliography of the Scholarship and Works* (Garland, 1976), *H. E. Bates* (Twayne, English Authors Series, no. 358, 1983), and an edited volume, *The English Short Story, 1945–1980, a Critical History* (Twayne, 1985). In addition, Vannatta has published articles on Alain Robbe-Grillet, Peter Handke, Max Apple, V. S. Pritchett, William Gass, Tim O'Brien, and James Dickey in *Modern Fiction Studies*, *The Literary Review*, and other books and journals. A short story writer himself, Vannatta has published fiction and poetry in a number of literary journals and little magazines. For the past several years, Vannatta has served as criticism editor of the literary journal *Crazyhorse*.

About the Editor

General editor Gordon Weaver earned his B.A. in English at the University of Wisconsin-Milwaukee in 1961; his M.A. in English at the University of Illinois, where he studied as a Woodrow Wilson Fellow, in 1962; and his Ph.D. in English and creative writing at the University of Denver in 1970. He is the author of several novels, including *Count a Lonely Cadence, Give Him a Stone, Circling Byzantium,* and most recently *The Eight Corners of the World* (Vermont: Chelsea Green Publishing Company, 1988). Many of his numerous short stories are collected in *The Entombed Man of Thule, Such Waltzing Was Not Easy, Getting Serious, Morality Play,* and *A World Quite Round.* For his fiction he has received the St. Lawrence Award for Fiction (1973), a National Endowment for the Arts fellowship (1974), and the O. Henry First Prize (1979). He edited *The American Short Story, 1945–1980: A Critical History.* He is a professor of English at Oklahoma State University and an adjunct member of the faculty of the Vermont College Master of Fine Arts Program in Writing. Married, and the father of three daughters, he lives in Stillwater, Oklahoma.